GW01451356

Soundings

A journal of politics and culture

Issue 42

The killing fields of inequality

Editor
Jonathan Rutherford

Managing Editor
Sally Davison

Founding Editors
Stuart Hall
Doreen Massey
Michael Rustin

Associate Editors
Geoff Andrews, Sarah Benton, Jo Littler

Reviews Editor
George Shire

Poetry Editor
Ruth Borthwick

Art Editor
Tim Davison

Editorial Office
Lawrence & Wishart, 99a Wallis Road, London E9 5LN

Advertisements
Write for information to Soundings, c/o Lawrence & Wishart

Subscriptions
2009 subscription rates are (for three issues):
UK: Institutions £82, Individuals £35
Rest of the world: Institutions £92.50,
Individuals £45

Collection as a whole © Soundings 2009
Individual articles © the authors 2009

No article may be reproduced or transmitted by any means, electronic or
mechanical, including photocopying, recording or any information storage and
retrieval system, without the permission in writing of the publisher,
editor or author

ISSN 1362 6620
ISBN 9781907103018

Cover Photo © GMB Akash/Panos Pictures

Printed in Great Britain by Biddles, Kings Lynn
Soundings is published three times a year, in autumn, spring and summer by:
Lawrence & Wishart, 99a Wallis Road, London E9 5LN.
Email: info@lwbooks.co.uk

www.soundings.org.uk

Contents

FREE TO VIEW
Ebooks From Soundings/L&W

The crash - a view from the left
Edited by Jon Cruddas and Jonathan Rutherford

The Crash offers an alternative to the compromised policies of dominant economics. Contributors analyse and explain the economic and social issues that lie at the heart of our crisis: the credit crisis, the housing disaster, secrecy jurisdictions, the practices of private equity firms and the intellectual failure of orthodox economics. They put forward ideas for a new kind of agriculture to ensure food security, a People's Post Bank, and a Green New Deal for tackling global warming; and make the case that Britain should think seriously about joining the Euro. And, taking a wider view, contributors identify historical trends in economic crashes, the immorality of inequality, and the arguments for a left alternative.

Contributors: *Jon Cruddas, Clive Dilnot, Bryan Gould, John Grahl, Colin Hines, Adam Leaver, Toby Lloyd, Lindsay Mackie, Robin Maynard, Richard Murphy, Carlota Perez, Ann Pettifor, Michael Prior, Jonathan Rutherford, Göran Therborn.*

Is the future conservative
Edited by Jon Cruddas and Jonathan Rutherford

The Conservative Party is now resurgent, attempting to reinvent its political traditions and preparing for power. But do their politics provide any answers to the challenges that lie ahead? What political direction might they take if they win the next election?

This collection brings together critical analysis of New Conservative thinking by writers from the left and right - including Neal Lawson, Oliver Letwin MP, Tony Juniper, John Harris and Tory thinker Phillip Blond.

For more free-to-view books and articles visit
www.lwbooks.co.uk/ebooks/ebooks.html

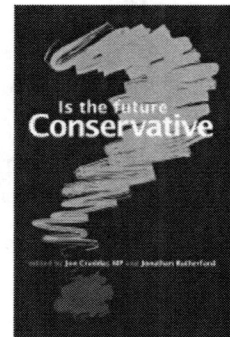

Editorial

The contemporary political scene is criss-crossed by systems of willed ignorance, the most obvious example being in the field of economics. The opening articles in this issue point to other areas where those in power - both in the UK and internationally - have turned their faces away from unpalatable reality. Julia Buxton describes how drugs policy remains impervious to research, continuing to focus on imprisoning minor players and importing conflict into drug-growing regions, while failing to address issues that lead problem users into addiction. Göran Therborn shows how inequality has its own killing fields - another social fact rarely acknowledged by those in power. And Jane Wills points to the ways in which multinational companies are able to abdicate from responsibility for their workers through systems of subcontracted employment: the system allows them to wash their hands of the consequent low wages paid out to the workforce, which are often below subsistence levels. Terry Wrigley, in his discussion of academies, discusses yet another area in which privatisation - which one would by now think to be well past its sell-by date as a policy option - is still seen as a viable means of running a public service (and Terry's article evidences some of the denials and fiddling of statistics that are required to maintain the fiction). The current distribution of power relies to a damaging extent on the powerful refusing to know the consequences of their actions.

Tim Dartington explores a different aspect of contemporary policy madness - the idea that health and welfare systems can be run on the basis of a repudiation of dependency. As Tim argues, this is closely connected to current concepts of the individual, and relationships between them: even in the public sphere relationships are reduced to transactional encounters between customers and suppliers. This is the context within which, for example, CBT can be offered as quick fix to all sorts of deeply embedded social problems. A concept of the individual imported from the world of commerce is driving out of the system any idea that people need looking after and kindness.

Guy Brown and Sarah Radcliffe discuss the unforeseen consequences of increasing lifespans, in that more people are now experiencing long periods of extremely poor health in the years before death. They put forward a number of ways of improving this situation, and these fit neatly alongside Hilary Cottam's discussion of Participle, a group working with older people in London. Participle is aiming to contribute to a major rethink of public services, based on a set of principles they call Beveridge 4.0. At the heart of this model is the notion that people want to be socially connected: this includes the idea that people want to contribute to their own well-being, but there is also a recognition of dependency. The suggestion is that social relationships are the key to renewing public services.

Elsewhere in the issue alternatives are discussed to current ways of thinking about our future food security; and Karel Williams shows how time frames and a sense of changing paradigms affect our understanding of the economy. Ben Little and Bryan Gould, in very different ways, reflect on our political future, while the reviews section focuses on an engagement with recent political interventions.

The UK drug problem in global perspective

Julia Buxton

The current international anti-drug model - subscribed to by the UK - results in far more harm than good.

――――

A mid recession and the credit crisis, one sector of the British economy continues to thrive - the trade in illicit drugs. Worth an estimated £5.3 billion, the booming UK drugs market is dynamic and ever expanding. Over the last decade it has made the UK a European leader in Class A drug consumption (cocaine, heroin and Ecstasy), cannabis use, home production of cannabis and in the numbers of 'harm causing' drug users. This is an inglorious domestic picture, and it is overlaid with a rise in drug-related violence and organised crime. But Britain's drug problem does not end here. Foreign policy engagement in Afghanistan and Colombia, the world's leading producers of opium and cocaine respectively, has coincided with a rise in both states in drug crop cultivation, drug manufacture and drug trafficking. This has financed insurgency in both countries, while undermining prospects for security, peace and development - the initial justification for UK military and financial assistance. The picture in Afghanistan is particularly dire. According to the United Nations World Drug Report, in 2001 - the year that the US led Operation Enduring Freedom was launched - Afghanistan produced 185 metric tonnes of opium. By 2007 the country was producing 8,200 metric tonnes, or 92 per cent of global opium supply. The sharpest rise in opium

7

poppy cultivation and opium production was in Helmand Province, the centre of UK deployment, which has received over £250 million in UK counter-narcotics assistance.

There is something clearly wrong with the UK's anti-drug strategy; and over the last decade increasingly cogent critiques of national drug policy have emerged. Articulated by think tanks and charities, academics and policy units, and by parliamentarians such as Paul Flynn, Harry Cohen, Lembit Opik and Evan Harris, these feed into a broader international wave of concern that the model of international drug control overseen by the UN through its Office on Drugs and Crime, and of which the UK is a part, is doing more harm than good. From this critical perspective, we are currently locked into an archaic international control model that has set unachievable goals, and which is counter-productive, anti-developmental, unjust and profoundly iatrogenic - the cure is worse than the disease. Those most harmed by current national and international strategy are the poor, the vulnerable and the socially marginalised, from Southern Afghanistan to Southern England. There is now growing pressure for a rethink of the guiding principles of drug control, principally from the countries of Latin America, Europe and Asia.

The urgency of reform has become all the more pressing since the end of the cold war. The narcotic drug trade has thrived in global free markets, prospering amid the deregulation of transport, finance, travel and employment. New markets and trafficking routes have opened up, with countries and regions such as the old Soviet block, China, the Caribbean and West Africa presenting lucrative new opportunities for illicit business expansion. The drugs trade has also become embedded in transnational crime and - after a fall off in superpower financing - 'narco' funding for insurgency, conflict, paramilitary violence and terrorism. A surge in HIV Aids infection linked to the injecting of heroin has followed in the trade's wake; an estimated 10 per cent of new global HIV infections are linked to injecting drug use. Environmental degradation due to illegal planting of drug crops and the production of cocaine and heroin has also increased exponentially. It is estimated that 600 million litres of chemicals are used annually in drug production in South America. According to the US Department of State, two metric tonnes of chemical waste is generated for every hectare of coca processed into cocaine in Peru. Figures released by the Colombian National Police show that conversion of one hectare of coca into cocaine base and cocaine requires 10 litres of sulphuric acid, 38 litres of acetone and 2 kilos of permanganate, and the total amount of gasoline required for annual cocaine production is equivalent to 6.8 days of gasoline consumption for the whole of the country. The current international control model, structured by 13 international conventions signed since 1912, but principally guided by the 1961 Single Convention on Narcotic Drugs, is simply not up to the task of addressing the new, more complex challenges of the modern world.

These are daunting times that require informed and objective debate. Unfortunately this shows no sign of emerging in the UK, where parliamentary discussion of drugs is naive, the recommendations of expert commissions are routinely rejected by policy-makers, and the majority of the print media propagate a strong, sensationalist anti-reform message. A reflective position on drugs is seen as a no-go for politicians and national government. As the Home Affairs committee noted in its Third Report, *The Government's Drug Policy: Is it Working?*: 'with a handful of brave exceptions ... drugs policy is an area where British politicians have feared to tread'. The end result is a vicious cycle of populist rhetoric, which panders to the prejudices and fears of a nation that is, by European standards, poorly educated about drugs. The recent national debate on the increase in cocaine use encapsulated this problem. MPs made a strong link between the rise in cocaine consumption and its (very public) use by celebrities. This view was echoed in the media, by the police and in government anti-drugs campaigns. Discussion of the main and more complex drivers of the increase, such as the fall in price and increased availability of supply, went largely ignored. As the UK was impacted by changing international supply routes and reconfigurations of the international supply chain, Kate Moss was the epicentre of our national debate on cocaine.

The international drug control model

The idea that nation states should work collectively together to limit the harm caused by intoxicating substances was first set out by US Evangelical Christian missionaries more than a century ago. They found the unregulated trade in opium - in which the UK had traditionally been the dominant actor - morally repugnant and an impediment to conversion in the South East Asian countries in which they were operating. After the US acquired the Philippines from Spain following its victory in the Spanish American war of 1898, the Roosevelt government came under strong pressure from the evangelical lobby to ban the retail trade in opium that had been operated by the Spanish in the territory. It conceded to these demands, and also to the missionaries' request that it should engage in 'narco-diplomacy' and convene an international conference to explore restrictions on the opium trade.

The principles and objectives of drug control that were set out by the US at the first international drug conference in Shanghai in 1909 frame the contemporary control system of today. These include the goal of prohibition - a world free from the cultivation, production, trafficking and consumption of harmful substances; criminalisation of the non-medical use and trade in harmful, controlled substances; and multilateral cooperation. From this has flowed an emphasis on punishment and enforcement in drug policy (thereby institutionalising the police and security services as the primary actors in drug control), underpinned by strategies that include the incarceration of individuals, forced eradication of drug crops and the destruction of production facilities and trafficking networks. Importantly, the orientation of drug control from the outset was towards supply rather than demand-side control. Eliminating the market in harmful and intoxicating substances was seen to be achievable by terminating the supply of opium poppy, coca and their derivative products at source in countries such as China, India, Turkey, the Balkans, Peru and Bolivia. The role of demand was not addressed, and with drug use simplistically conceptualised as a failure of moral will, repression was prioritised over treatment and prevention.

Approaches framed in a period of colonialism, racism and Social Darwinism, and before the professionalisation of medicine, still shape the international response to the complex globalised drug markets of the contemporary period. Across the course of the last one hundred years, there has been no revisiting of these basic concepts. On the contrary, the six international drug control conventions and protocols that came into force during the inter-war period, and the seven that followed after the second world war, have reasserted and reinforced founding assumptions. This is deeply problematic given the accumulation of evidence that a drug-free world is an unrealisable objective, and that the costs of continuing to pursue it far outweigh any net attainable benefits.

Prohibition as utopia

Civilisations have ingested intoxicating and hallucinogenic drugs for thousands of years. With the exception of the Inuit, all societies have a social and cultural history of drug use. This has prompted anthropologists to consider the extent to which the desire for 'out of body' experiences is as innate to human nature as breathing, sex and eating. The US-led puritan drive for abstinence and godliness sits uncomfortably alongside this reality of human enquiry and free will. For it is arguable that achieving prohibition would require a fundamental transformation of society and individuals, a goal that is impossible to achieve without social reprogramming or brutally intensive surveillance.

Aside from debates over human nature and freedom of choice, a more fundamental problem with prohibition is that it is trumped by basic market forces. Consider the following. Coca, opium poppy and cannabis are essentially weeds and shrubs that are easy to produce and which can be cultivated in the most marginal of environments. Prohibiting them (except for medical and scientific research) has served to create a flourishing illicit market, which is unregulated, which cannot be taxed, and in which contracts can only be enforced through violence or the threat of violence. Today's illicit trade is estimated to be worth $94 billion at the wholesale level and $322 billion at the retail level. This is higher than the GDP of all sub-Saharan African countries combined, and the figure is larger than the total global market for meat ($52.5 billion), tobacco ($21.6 billion) and coffee ($5.7 billion). The incentives to engage in the illicit trade are high, particularly for the estimated 4 million men, women and children who are engaged in drug crop cultivation because of poverty, marginalisation and insecurity. At all levels of the illicit drug chain, engagement in production, trafficking and distribution is more lucrative and reliable than employment in the formal economy. The risks are high, but the rewards are substantial.

It is precisely because of the profit incentives generated by the illegality of drugs that any one step forward, or short-term success, in the 'war on drugs' leads to two steps backwards and long-term defeat. The market logic here is simple. Programmes to eradicate drug crops, such as the US-sponsored Plan Colombia in Colombia, or seizures of drug trans-shipments, have the effect of reducing supply. This in turn drives prices up, increasing the incentive for new sources to come into a global market characterised by low entry costs and few barriers. This reality contradicts the flawed premise of drug control, that supply reductions will drive up cost, thereby making drugs unaffordable for users and leading to market collapse. In the UK, where we have laboured under the illusion that enforcement is effective, ever-increasing custom seizures (for example, the doubling of Class A drug seizures in England and Wales between 1996 and 2005) have had no impact on price, purity or availability. UK drug markets, as with drug markets in other countries of the world, have proved resilient, adaptive and impervious to law enforcement.

A related problem here is the 'balloon effect'. Because of the price incentives in the illicit trade, successful suppression in one area causes the trade to be displaced, resurfacing elsewhere. Squeezing the trade is just like squeezing a balloon - the drugtrade, like the air in a balloon, simply pops up elsewhere. This phenomenon has been observed repeatedly in all areas of the drug trade chain. The end result - and the situation that we inherit in the current period - is one of fragmentation of the illicit market, which has become more complex and more difficult to control.

For example, and starting with the cultivation of drug crops, 'success' in reducing opium cultivation in the traditional producer states of the Golden Triangle (Thailand, Myanmar and Laos) in the 1970s and 1980s has been offset by a rise in cultivation and production in the Golden Crescent (Pakistan and more specifically Afghanistan). Similarly, coca cultivation eradication exercises in Peru and Bolivia served only to shift the locus of the cocaine trade to Colombia. This ballooning is observable within, as well as between, states. For example, progress in reducing opium poppy cultivation in Northern Afghanistan has led to the relocation of cultivation to the country's Southern provinces. In Colombia, reductions in coca cultivation in the traditional growing areas of Putumayo, Norte de Santander and Guaviare has been countered by rising cultivation in Boyaca, Meta, Antioquia and Bolivar. And the balloon effect in cultivation also helps to account for the surge in the home cultivation of cannabis in the UK. Traditionally, the British cannabis market has been supplied by cultivating states such as Morocco, Lebanon and Afghanistan. However, success in reducing supply from these countries (through customs seizures in the UK and the provision of development assistance to the source countries) led to a decline the availability of cannabis. This was rapidly filled by home production, with the use of hydroponic growing kits and imported seeds. A study by South Bank University's Criminal Policy Research Unit and the National Addiction Centre at King's College London, estimated that as much as half of the cannabis consumed in England and Wales may now be grown here. And in contrast to the milder forms of cannabis, with lower psychoactive THC content, that was previously imported from overseas, home-produced cannabis is stronger and more potent, as a result of economies of scale and seed supply. So while Moroccan cannabis has a THC content of about 5 per cent, UK grown skunk has a 15 per cent THC content.

Ballooning in cultivation patterns has had knock-on implications for drug trafficking routes and trafficking organisations. It has enabled geographically dispersed actors to enter the illicit trade while opening up new and populous markets. For example, with the centralisation of opium and heroin production in Afghanistan in the 1990s and 2000s, Central Asia, the Balkans and eastern European countries emerged as new corridors of access to buoyant Western European markets, with ethnic ties and migration patterns transforming organisational and trafficking structures across continents. These transit regions have also become important consumer states in their own right, part of a new post cold war trend of drug consumption increasing in developing countries that were formerly insulated from the trade. Problematically, this pattern of displacement and fragmentation has been accelerated by enforcement efforts. A cogent example here is the situation in the cocaine markets. In an effort to halt the traffic of cocaine (as well as cannabis and heroin) from South to North America, US counter-narcotics efforts over recent years have focused on sealing the transit corridors in Central America, and, with the help of the UK Royal Navy, the Caribbean. The impact of this strategy has been a reorientation of drug trafficking routes. These now run from Colombia, through Venezuela and Brazil, to West Africa. From the poor, fragile and post-conflict states in this region, the drug then transits to markets in Europe through entry points in Spain and the Netherlands. This, rather than Kate Moss's social life, is the context of the UK cocaine 'surge'.

Just as eliminating one supply source or transit route creates a plethora of new ones, so eliminating a major cartel or trafficking gang creates space for rivals. Over the last two decades, international drug control agencies have enjoyed success in removing drug 'king pins' such as Pablo Escobar in Colombia, Khun Sa in Myanmar and Gulbuddin Hekmatyar in Afghanistan. But this has had no impact on volumes of traffic. On the contrary, the volume has increased, as large, hierarchical organisations have been supplanted by smaller, more compact, agile and diffusely organised supercartelitos or boutique cartels, which criss-cross the globe and which are intermeshed with transnational criminal organisations. Running parallel with this, there has been a sharp rise in drug-related violence, as smaller gangs fight for control of market share, and as the lines of authority and control, which were traditionally exercised by major cartels, disintegrate. Mexico is a tragic example of the disintegration and bloodshed that ensues from conflict between rival factions competing for lucrative illicit market share. In the last year, more than 5700 people have been killed in drug-related violence in the country, a doubling of the drug-related mortality figures recorded in 2007. According to Adam Thompson, writing in the *Financial Times*, the trafficking market in Mexico is worth some $13.8 billion ('Mexico helpless as drugs war rages', *FT* 4.12.08). Efforts by US and Mexican authorities to curtail the traffic through military force, as financed by the US-sponsored Merida Initiative, have served only to exacerbate the violence. In Mexico, as in countries as diverse as Brazil, Thailand, Sierra Leone, the US and the UK, trafficking gangs have responded to state violence by increasing their own defensive capabilities. The end result is a chronic deterioration in security and stability.

In terms of consumption, the drug control model has also proved utterly ineffective. More people are consuming drugs today than at any point in the previous one hundred years. There are an estimated 165 million cannabis users worldwide, 23.7 million ATS users, 16 million cocaine users and 16 million opiate users (of which 11 million are heroin users). More woman consume drugs today than ever before, people are initiated into drug use at a younger age, and drug 'careers' now last longer. In sum, drugs are no longer something that rich, white, young western males briefly experiment with before their entry into the responsible world of marriage and work - as was the case in the 1960s. Consumption patterns have proved remarkably adaptive and resilient. Punitive responses, as outlined in the international conventions and implemented through national legislative frameworks, have had no impact on drug use or intention to use. Moreover, enforcement - and eliminating the supply of one type of drug - has not reduced overall consumption levels. The increase in prices resulting from a shortage of supply rarely acts as a deterrent to purchase and consumption, undermining a key premise of the control system. When it does, users simply switch to a different drug (such as amphetamine), or, as in the case of heroin, dependent users turn to acquisitive crime in order to increase their purchasing power. This explains the often observed pattern in UK communities of successful drug raids generating an increase in crime, drug-related violence and ultimately the local supply of drugs.

'Successful' enforcement against drug users and distributors also has serious and negative public health impacts. For example, a diminution of supply typically leads to the 'cutting' or dilution of drugs such as heroin with other (sometimes lethal) substances. As a result of prohibition approaches, users are already ignorant of the content, quality and quantity of the drugs that they are ingesting; and market disruption serves only to heighten susceptibility to illness, infection, overdose and death. Similarly, 'clampdowns' on users through stop and search techniques also increase the risk of individual and public harm. Heroin users tend not to carry injecting equipment if they think they may be approached by the police. This in turn results in increased sharing of needles, which results in a heightened risk of HIV Aids, Hepatitis B and C and other blood born diseases.

More harm than good

As discussed at the beginning of this article, the impacts of unsuccessful drug control are disproportionately born by the most vulnerable sections of global society. Despite growing evidence of the regressive and counterproductive effects of drug policy, the UN Office for Drugs and Crime has significantly failed to address or mitigate these impacts; the international community remains wedded to a model that exacerbates problems of underdevelopment, poverty, social breakdown and deprivation. Some factual examples illustrate this argument.

The bulk of counter narcotics spending continues to be focused on enforcement and interdiction, in line with the supply orientation of the Christian missionary lobby a century ago: it is security sector agencies (private and public sector) that benefit from the bulk of counter-narcotics financing. Demand-side issues - such as treatment, rehabilitation, education and prevention - suffer a deficit in spending, even though these interventions have been repeatedly shown to be more cost effective and successful in reducing drug use. According to the Rand Corporation, $12 has to be spent on enforcement to have the equivalent effect to $1 spent on treatment.

The UK currently spends roughly equal amounts on enforcement and treatment: a 2003 report by the Prime Minister's Strategy Unit put the allocation of spending at £480 million per year on demand prevention and £450 million on reducing the supply of class A drugs (monies to the police, Serious Organised Crime Agency, Customs and Excise, etc). In the US, the world's leading consumer nation, 70 per cent of federal resources are ring-fenced for supply-focused activities and just 30 per cent for demand-side initiatives. But the supply-side orientation has failed to reduce the supply of drugs, in part because it does not address the profit incentives to engage in supply but also because enforcement activities are disproportionately directed at the least important elements of the drug chain: peasant cultivators, petty dealers and drug addicts. For example, in the UK, 74 per cent of heroin seizures, 70 per cent of crack seizures and 61 per cent of cocaine seizures between 1996 and 2005 were of less than one gram in weight. Further to this, supply-focused activities (drug crop eradication, interdiction) are concentrated in source countries. However, the value of the global illicit market at the producer levels is just $12.8 billion. The majority of profits - an estimated 90 per cent - is realised at the wholesale and retail end. The value of drugs such as cocaine and heroin increases by a staggering 2412 per cent between the farm gate in Colombia and Afghanistan and the consumers in the UK and the US. And yet it is the source countries that are the focus of intelligence, eradication and interdiction efforts.

Moreover the impact of these external interventions in source countries is deeply problematic and structurally imbalanced. The majority of drug crop cultivators are impoverished and marginalised peasants, whose livelihoods and security depend on drug crop cultivation in the absence of legitimate, viable economic alternatives. However, addressing the development needs of these communities has not been a primary concern for the UNODC or consumer nations, despite rhetoric of shared responsibility. Financing for alternative development programmes that would allow for the integration of cultivating communities into the formal economy on a sustainable basis has been chronically low. The bulk of funding continues to be reserved for (Western-defined) security imperatives, to the detriment of source country development. The most notorious example of this skewing of budgets is the US sponsored Plan Colombia, which was launched by US president Bill Clinton in 1999. Of the initial budget allocation of $1.6 billion, just 8 per cent was dedicated to development and justice sector reform. The remainder was allocated to the military and police for training, weapons purchases and enforcement activities. A similar pattern is observable in Afghanistan, where UK and international assistance for alternative development has been massively overshadowed by security sector support and technical training. This is justified on the basis that security has to be established in order to create an enabling environment and entry points for development assistance.

The UK drug problem in global perspective

The fundamental flaw here is that ongoing cultivation finances insurgency and conflict, in turn increasing pressures to allocate more funding to the security sector. In addition, the type of security support financed and proffered by countries such as the UK is 'hard' security, focused on strengthening a weak and usually illegitimate state. It does not focus on 'soft' security', which is to say the localised security needs of cultivators. In this context, efforts to eliminate drug crops through strategies of forced eradication have served only to increase cultivator support for insurgent groups, which are seen as the protectors of cultivator security, interests and livelihoods.

Another example relates to trafficking. It is increasingly recognised that the majority of arrested 'mules' and smugglers coming into the UK are typically poor young women, single mothers from poorer countries. These are operators on the lowest rung of the smuggling chain, increasingly used by trafficking gangs in order to minimise the risk of bulk consignment seizure. The majority are unaware of the severity of the penalties that they face on arrest (up to fourteen years imprisonment), and when they are incarcerated in foreign jails their children are left vulnerable and sometimes abandoned back in the home country. But it is to be noted that the UK spends five times more money imprisoning female mules from Jamaica than it allocates to the country in development assistance.

The issue of imprisonment also leads to debate around the utility and impacts of criminalisation. The punishment and incarceration of drug 'offenders' has damaging implications for their families, their children and their own long-term opportunities, particularly for the majority of drug users, who are non-problematic, occasional consumers. Imprisonment is also morally and medically questionable in relation to drug addicts. Chronic limitations in referral and support services mean that prisons internationally are not positioned to offer treatment or support to drug users, or assistance in breaking the cycle of damaging and problem behaviour that drives problem drug use and crime. In the UK, for example, where drug-related crime costs an estimated £13.5 billion per year, the UK Drug Policy Commission found in its March 2008 report *Reducing Drug Use, Reducing Offending*, that 1 in 8 arrestees (equivalent to about 125,000 people in England and Wales) were problem heroin and/or crack users, compared with 1 in 100 of the general population. Of arrestees who used heroin and/or crack at least once a week, 81 per cent said they had committed an acquisitive crime in the previous 12 months, compared with 30 per cent of other arrestees. One third reported an average of at least one crime a day. In recognition of the link between problem drug use (by a small minority of drug users) and crime, the UK government has placed more emphasis on treatment and integrated referral services in its last two Ten Year Drug strategy papers. Investment in prison treatment in England and Wales increased from £7 million in 1997/98 to £80 million in 2007/08; the number of prisoners on maintenance-prescribing or detoxification programmes in prison in England and Wales increased from under 14,000 in 1996/97 to over 51,500 in 2006/07; and there are now a number of integrated interventions available. However, the UKDPC found that prison drug services: 'fall short of even minimum standards', and new strategies had been poorly monitored. As a result: 'we know remarkably little about what works and for whom'.

Community provision is also well below need. In its 2003 report, the Prime Minister's Strategy Unit put the number of harm causing problematic users at 280,000 (mainly heroin and crack consuming) people, causing £5bn of health and social harm and £16bn of crime harm - including 80 per cent of burglaries, 54 per cent of robberies and 45 per cent of fraud. Each user was estimated to cause £75,000 of harm each year, of which £60,000 was crime related. Only 20 per cent of these 'harm causing' drug users were in treatment, and of the 130,000 problematic drug users that entered the criminal justice system, only 17,000 ended up in treatment. The Home Affairs committee concluded its enquiry into the government's drug strategy by stating that General Practitioners 'are, for the most part, inadequately trained to deal with drug misuse'.

While efforts to address treatment needs should be welcomed, a sobering concluding finding is that, according to the RSA Drugs Commission Report of 2007 (*Drugs: Facing the Facts*), those most vulnerable to problematic drug use in the UK are those who have been in care, in trouble with the police, excluded from school, or who are unemployed or homeless (one in three problem drug users are homeless or in need of housing support). Nearly two-thirds of female drug users contacting treatment services had been physically abused, and more than one-third sexually abused by a family member or family friend. Given this, an alternative approach to current strategy would be one that addressed problematic drug use through social investment, effective welfare provision and employment creation, not incarceration.

The UK drug problem in global perspective

Deprivation, not deviance, is the driver of our current national drug 'problem'.

Conclusion

Stricter, tighter and better enforcement of drug laws, as frequently called for by backbenchers, cabinet ministers and government officials, simply will not work. There needs to be a realistic and comprehensive re-examination of the guiding principles of drug control, and serious questioning of the workings of the UNODC. Informed, evidence-based analysis, which locates the UK drug problem in global context, needs to be brought to the table, and policy responses must be more attuned to the factors of poverty, inequality and exclusion that drive the illicit trade. At a more basic level, it has to be recognised that it is only the illegality of cheap shrubs and weeds that makes them so lucrative and destabilising. Nothing epitomises the tragic failure of officials and elected representatives to get to grips with the challenges we face than the recent, absurd debate on the reclassification of cannabis from a class C to a class B drug. That, and Jacqui Smith's arrogant dismissal of the Advisory Council on the Misuse of Drugs recommendations, demonstrates how far we have to go in having an informed public debate, and the seriousness of the threats that officials expose us to.

The killing fields of inequality

Göran Therborn

What are the contemporary causes of inequality in the world?

——

There are three main ways of distinguishing between difference and inequality. First, a difference may be horizontal, without anything or anybody being higher or lower, better or worse, whereas an inequality is always vertical, or involves ranking. Secondly, differences are matters of taste and/or of categorisation only. An inequality, on the other hand, is not just a categorisation; it is something that violates a moral norm of equality among human beings. (To argue this is not to presuppose any norm of complete equality, but to point to a difference that is too big and/or has an undeserved direction, i.e. the wrong people getting the best rewards.) Thirdly, for a difference to become an inequality it must also be abolishable. The greater physical prowess of the average 20-year-old in comparison with the average 60-year-old is not an inequality. But the different social life-chances of women as compared to men, or of black working-class boys in comparison with white bankers' boys, have come to be seen as inequalities. In one sentence: inequalities are avoidable, morally unjustified, hierarchical differences.

There are (at least) three fundamentally different kinds of inequality, and all of them are destructive of human lives and of human societies.

There is inequality of health and death, which we may call *vital inequality*. True, we are all mortal and physically vulnerable, and in some sense our life-tree is decided by some inscrutable lottery. However, hard evidence is piling up that health and longevity are distributed with clearly visible social patterns. Children in

The killing fields of inequality

poor countries and poor classes die more often before the age of one, and between the age of one and five, than children in rich countries and rich classes. Low-status people in Britain die more often before retirement age than high-status people, and if they survive have shorter lives in retirement. A retired British male bank or insurance employee, for instance, can look forward to seven to eight more years of retirement life than a retired employee of Whitbread or Tesco (*Financial Times*, 20/21.10.07). Vital inequality, which we can measure relatively easily through life expectancy and survival rates, is literally destroying millions of human lives in the world every year.

Existential inequality hits you as a person. It restricts the freedom of action of certain categories of persons, for instance of women in public spaces and spheres, as in Victorian and Edwardian Britain, and as in some countries still today. Existential inequality means denial of (equal) recognition and respect, and is a potent generator of humiliations, for black people, (Amer-)Indians, women in patriarchal societies, poor immigrants, low castes and stigmatised ethnic groups. It is important to note here that existential inequality does not only take the form of blatant discrimination; it also operates effectively through more subtle status hierarchies.

Thirdly, there is *material* or resource *inequality*, meaning that human actors have very different resources to draw upon. We can distinguish two aspects here. The first is inequality of *access* - to education, career tracks and social contacts, to what is called 'social capital'. In conventional mainstream discussions this aspect is often referred to as 'inequality of opportunity'. The second is inequality of *rewards*, often referred to as inequality of outcome. This is the most frequently used measure of inequality - the distribution of income, sometimes also of wealth.

These three kinds of inequality interact with and influence each other. But it is useful to distinguish between them because, as well as having different types of effects on people, the different kinds of inequality have different trajectories in different periods - which means that they are governed by different causal mechanisms.

Inequality can be produced in four basic ways. First there is *distantiation* - some people are running ahead and/or others falling behind. Secondly there is the mechanism of *exclusion* - through which a barrier is erected making it impossible, or at least more difficult, for certain categories of people to access a good life. Thirdly, the institutions of *hierarchy* mean that societies and organisations are constituted as ladders, with some people perched on top and others below. Finally, there is *exploitation*, in which the riches of the rich derive from the toil and the subjection of the poor and the disadvantaged.

The historical importance of these mechanisms in generating the configuration of the modern world is hotly disputed. Are current inequalities primarily a product of North Atlantic nations forging ahead, through scientific and industrial innovations? Or are they rather an effect of exclusion, for example the British empire's hindering of Indian industry from developing? Did the 'modern world system' after 1500 spawn a world hierarchy of a core, a semi-periphery, and periphery? Or was the rise of the West mainly driven by armed exploitation, by the plunder of American metals, by plantation slavery, and by forced and underpaid commodity production in the South? The debate remains unfinished, both because of the ambiguity of the evidence - there is empirical support for all four mechanisms, but it is difficult to weigh them in relation to each other - and because of the high moral historical stakes involved.

In this article, however, we shall look into the ways in which current inequalities are being produced.

Exploitation

Exploitation is not the direct cause in the case of vital inequality - the health of the healthy is not based upon the disease and death of others. But there is a clearly discernible path from the exploitation of workers in risky and unhealthy jobs for profit to inequality of health and life expectancy. For example mining in South Africa, China and the Ukraine, and, more generally, factory work in the 'Special Economic Zones' all over the world, are notorious for the deleterious effects they have on life and health. But this is only part of the picture. Chinese men have the same life expectancy as Poles, and live eight years longer than less industrialised Indians.

Existential inequality in the form of exploitative patriarchy has in general been on radical retreat in the world in the last three decades, even if occasionally hitting back, as in Afghanistan from the time of the anti-Communist jihad in the 1980s and thereafter. But, for example, the widespread West Asian notion, very strong in Chechnya, Kurdistan and Afghanistan, that a man's honour depends on the subordination and seclusion of his sisters, his wife (or wives), his daughters and his mother remains a generator of this form of inequality for many.

If you are not convinced of the labour theory of value, it is difficult to say how much economic inequality is due to capitalist exploitation. The drastic increase of income inequality in China recently, now much larger than in India or in Russia, is clearly significantly related to the capitalist use of cheap labour. But the increasing gap between Africa and the rest of the world is not caused by Africa being increasingly exploited. Nor can much of the widening gap between rich and poor in the US and UK be attributed to the increasing exploitation of workers, although the massive influx of cheap immigrant labour into the US has generated a polarised labour market, including the return of a servants' class, or 'service class', serving a so-called 'creative class'.

Exploitation - the most repulsive generator of inequality - can thus be seen as a significant driver of inequality in today's world, but it is not the major force.

Hierarchy

Overt hierarchy has been the object of attack by management gurus for quite some time now, and many organisations have been 'flattened'. Historically, rights of subordinates have been strengthened, including rights of collective representation - in continental European public and private management, and more widely in educational establishments. Against this trend, the countervailing powers of trade unions are generally declining.

The main point, however, is that even when organisational pyramids are flattened, organisations and societies at large are permeated by subtle hierarchies of social status. Through the unequal allocation of recognition and respect, the existence of different degrees of freedom to act, and the effects of hierarchies of self-respect and self-confidence, social-status hierarchies appear to be a major underlying reason for persistent inequalities of health and life expectancy. Social hierarchies produce existential inequality, which in turn has serious psycho-somatic consequences.

Although there was substantial income equalisation in countries such as the UK in the course of the twentieth century, class differentials of life expectancy have widened, particularly among men. In 1910-12 an unskilled manual worker in England and Wales had a 61 per cent greater risk of dying between the age of 20 and 44 than a professional man. In 1991-93 the extra risk of early adult death had risen to 186 per cent. For a semi-skilled worker the extra mortality risk was 6 per cent before the first world war and 76 per cent in the early 1990s.[1] The hardest evidence for the lethal effects of status hierarchies is probably Sir Michael Marmot's study of 18,000 Whitehall civil servants.[2] For this group of workers the risk of early death closely followed the office hierarchy. During the 25 years of study - after age, smoking, blood pressure, cholesterol concentration and a few other such factors had been controlled for - coronary heart disease killed 50 per cent more of those at the bottom of the hierarchy than those at the top (p45).

Exclusion

Barriers of exclusion have generally been lowered in the world in the last fifty years, though here too the picture is mixed. Exclusion of women from public space, from labour markets, and career ladders, has lessened in many parts of the world. Racism has become widely discredited; and the dismantling of South African apartheid, as well as the election of a Dalit state Prime Minister in India and an Afro-American President in the USA, are important landmarks. 'First Nations' of the Americas are finally being included into the national polities, including the recent achievement of winning their democratically deserved central place in Bolivia. The late twentieth century return to the mass migration of one hundred years before also means more inclusion. And regaining national sovereignty after the second world war ended the exclusion of China and India from possibilities of development. Between 1913 and 1950 the rate of economic growth in China and India was approximately zero. But between 1950 and 1973 Chinese growth was 4.9 per cent a year, and India's 3.5 per cent.[3] In recent decades, access to the US market has been a major engine of East Asian growth and of global equalisation.

However, though lowered, exclusion remains a major feature of the contemporary world, divided as it is into exclusive nation-states, each with its specific rights for citizens only. And there are also other excluding processes at work, including widespread trade protectionism, for example American cotton protectionism, which hits poor countries of the African savannah. In the current crisis, though there is an official taboo on protectionism, national exclusivism is

The killing fields of inequality

becoming more marked, as in 'British jobs for British workers' and 'Buy American'.

Distantiation

When it comes to the production of inequality through distantiation we are facing a paradox of our times. In a territorial sense, distances have shrunk enormously. Electronic communication and satellite transmission make it possible for the whole world to watch the Olympics or the Obama inauguration at the same time, and for friends in, say, China and Argentina or Mozambique and Canada to talk to each other on the phone. By email you can communicate with colleagues in Italy (hardly possible with Italian pre-electronic mail) as well as in Bangladesh. Existential distances, between 'races' or ethnicities, and between men and women, have also decreased, as we noticed above. But income and vital distances are increasing, between different parts of the world and within many countries.

In the first half of the 1970s, the distance in life expectancy at birth between sub-Saharan Africa and high-income countries was 25.5 years; thirty years later it was thirty years.[4] In the UK the life expectancy gap between the rich and the poor has been increasing by 0.15 years annually since the 1980s.[5] Within metropolitan Glasgow the gap between males in Calton and in Lenzie is 28 years, larger than that between the UK and Africa in the 1970s. Glaswegians from Calton have a shorter life expectancy than Australian Aborigines.[6] Capitalist Russia and the rest of the former Soviet Union are also falling behind in life prospects. In the early 1970s - the period of Communist 'stagnation' - the life expectancy gap in relation to high-income countries was 2.5 years; in the mid-2000s it is almost fifteen years.[7]

In 1973 GDP per capita in sub-Saharan Africa was about eight per cent of America's. In 2005 it had dropped to 5 per cent (measured in terms of domestic purchasing power).[8] In the US, the share of total household income appropriated by the richest 1 per cent was 8 per cent in 1980 and 17 per cent in 2000. In the UK the richest 1 per cent leapt from receiving 6 per cent of all income in 1980 to taking about 12.5 per cent in 2000;[9] and income after tax for those in the 99th percentile was 10.2 times bigger than for those in the 10th percentile in 1997-98, but 12.8 times bigger in 2006-7.[10]

The gap in income between those at the top and the average worker is now much wider than it was in pre-modern times. In 1688 English baronets had an annual income about one hundred times higher than that of labourers and out-servants, and 230 times that of cottagers and paupers. In 2007-8, chief executives of the FTSE top 100 companies received remuneration 141 times higher than the median income of all full-time employees in the UK, and 236 times higher than those of people in 'sales and customer service occupations'.[11]

Another angle from which to view the new economic distance is to look at the current world distribution of wealth. In March 2008, before the bubble burst, *Forbes* magazine listed 1125 billionaires in the world. Together they owned $4.4 trillion. That was almost the whole national income of 128 million Japanese, or a third of that of 302 million Americans. By March 2009 the billionaire numbers had decreased to 793, owning only $2.4 trillion - but that is still equal to the national income of France.[12]

Distantiation is the main road to increasing inequality today. It is the most subtle of mechanisms, the one most difficult to pin down morally and politically. Though its effects are highly visible in ostentatious consumption, it operates more through stealth than through assailable principles, or blatant violations of human rights. But distantiation is a mechanism or a channel of inequality; it is not a causal force. So what drives it? (It should be underlined at this point that distantiation is very rarely a product of extremely hard work or singular merit; it mainly results from windows of opportunity and networks of contact, or, conversely, from pre-given odds and social isolation.)

One reason for the growth in distance in vital inequality across the globe is that some countries have fallen behind. Sub-Saharan Africa has seen its life expectancy drop because of AIDS, which for reasons still not fully understood has hit Africa harder than any other area of the planet. Russia and the former Soviet Union, on the other hand, are victims of a ruthless restoration of capitalism, which has caused massive unemployment, economic insecurity, impoverishment and existential humiliation. Michael Marmot has estimated the death toll of capitalist restoration in Russia in the 1990s to be about four million people.[13] Within rich countries such as the UK, the growing life expectancy gap seems to be more an outcome of the privileged moving ahead, perhaps because they are more open to healthy lifestyle campaigns, and are under less existential stress. It should be kept in mind, though, that Marmot's Whitehall study showed that correlation of low status and premature death persisted after controls for smoking, cholesterol and other 'lifestyle' indicators.

The killing fields of inequality

The global increase in income gap is again mainly an effect of Africa falling behind. But here the reasons are more obscure and contested than in the case of mortality. The continent is politically fragmented and logistically weakly connected, and is heavily dependent on international commodity markets that are outside its control; and the disruption of its political traditions by colonial partitions-turned-nation-states laid the basis for what have frequently become dysfunctional national polities, in many cases aggravated by cold war and 'structural adjustment' interventions. The impoverishment of the former Soviet Union and the late twentieth-century crisis decades in Latin America have also added to the increasing distance between levels of income across the globe.

In contrast to these cases where people and countries are falling behind, the widening gap in intra-national income is driven mainly from the top - although in the US (but not in the UK, at least not until the year of 2006/7-2007/8, when British capitalism also impoverished the poor[14]) the soaring of the highest incomes in the last decade was also accompanied by a slow decline in the income of the poorest fifth of the population. That the top is now running ahead rather than the poor falling behind means that competition from low-wage countries is a minor component of the gap. Interestingly, the u-turn in income inequality is primarily an Anglo-Saxon phenomenon, most pronounced in the US, but also marked in Canada, the UK, Australia, and New Zealand. It cannot be described as a consequence of modern times, since it has not been so much of a trend in Germany, France, Netherlands, and Switzerland.[15]

What has driven the enormous widening of economic distances among people in the last decades? There seem to have been two major processes at work.

One is the extension of solvent markets, which has increased both the pool of rewards and the competition for 'star talent'. A small business elite has been catapulted upwards, surfing on the soaring stock markets that were sustained by the lifting of controls on capital movements in the 1980s and the expansion of transnational investment, and profiting from the emergence of a global executive and professional market. A similar phenomenon has occurred in sports and entertainment (something that is increasingly discussed in apologetics for inequality); commercial television and satellite broadcasting have transformed the economics of sports and entertainment in general, while hugely expanded audiences widen the visibility and attraction of stars, augment the remuneration pool and increase profits. Entertainment capitalism and stardom symbiotically feed off each other.

The second factor was the trend towards the increased autonomy of financial capitalism from what is still called 'the real economy', a process particularly pronounced in Wall Street and the City and their other Anglo-Saxon emulators. In the last ten years this has turned capitalist finance into a gigantic gambling casino, which trades in currencies, 'securities' and 'derivatives'. The amount of nominal money involved has become astronomical. In early March 2009 the Asian Development Bank estimated that in the current crisis the value of financial assets in the world had by then fallen by up to $50,000bn - which is a figure equal to the total value of the world product in 2007.[16] For as long as the balloon was ascending the losers were few, and unless you were caught doing something outright illegal you could be sure that you would be handsomely rewarded even if you lost. The bonus culture was rewarding immediate expansion, and was not bothered about later losses.

It is noteworthy that in the US and the UK, as finance was distancing itself from the rest of the economy, it was simultaneously moving closer to (admittedly very relative) left-of-centre politics. In the final stages of the 2008 US Presidential campaign, conservative columnist David Brooks noted sadly in the *New York Times* that investment bankers were 2:1 for Obama. In the UK, the Blair-Brown governments have been happily surrounded by sympathetic City bankers. What do the high gamblers and the New Democrats and New Labour have in common? - a common contempt for industrial society, with its working-class collectivism and its bourgeois values of work, thrift, and restraint?

Inequality, so what?

OK, inequality is a fact, and increasing, so what? Does it matter if David Beckham earns much more than you do? (Tony Blair on one occasion appeared to offer this question as a cover for leaving income inequality untouched.)

My answer is that it does matter, because inequality is a violation of human rights; the invocation of celebrity pay is simply a smoke-screen.

Few people are likely to argue that a society which awards 28 fewer years of life to people in the most disadvantaged neighbourhood (Glasgow Calton) than to those in the most privileged ones (Glasgow Lenzie, London Kensington and Chelsea) is a decent society. Is it a vindication of the superiority of capitalism that male life expectancy in capitalist Russia is now seventeen years shorter than in Cuba?[17] Social status hierarchies are, literally, lethal. Why should those on the lowest rungs of the Whitehall ladder have a four times higher likelihood of dying before retirement age than those on the top rungs? The USA - the richest country on earth, and the most unequal among the rich countries - has the third highest rate of relative poverty of all the 30 OECD countries (after Mexico and Turkey). Such relative poverty means being excluded from many parts of the social and cultural life of your society. But the US also scores badly on absolute poverty rates: the poorest tenth of the US population has an income well below the average poor of the OECD; the income of this group in the US is lower than that of the poorest tenth in Greece.[18]

The transformation of capitalist finance into a huge global casino is what has created the current economic crisis, which has put hundreds of thousands out of employment and led to demands for billions of pounds of taxpayers' money. In the South the world crisis is bringing more poverty, hunger, and death. The effects of run-away distantiation are no longer defensible - if they ever were - by reference to fans' infatuation with their indulged stars.

The stretching social distance between the poorest and the richest diminishes social cohesion, which in turn means more collective problems - such as crime and violence - and fewer resources for solving all our other collective problems, from national identity to climate change. Western Europe - east of the British Isles, west of Poland, and north of the Alps - is still the world's least inegalitarian area, and has relatively high levels of social cohesion. For an experience of the full power of inequalities, you should look at the violence and fear of many South African and Latin American cities.

What is to be done?

While explicitly refusing the mantle of the politician or the prophet, there are a few things an expatriate scholar might venture to say.

Global inequality is to a large extent class and intra-state ethnic inequality. While overall income inequality is still governed by nation-state divisions, class and ethnic demarcations are cutting through them. As we learnt above, intra-Glasgow inequality of life expectancy in the 2000s superseded the gap between the UK and sub-Saharan Africa in the 1970s. Comparing international figures through the 'top-to-bottom' ratio (the ratio between the top ten per cent and the bottom ten per cent of a given group), we see that the ratio between the richest and poorest 10 per cent of the world's population in terms of average GDP per capita was 39 in 2005. However, large gaps exist within nations as well as between them. In Brazil the top-to-bottom ratio in 2005 was 48; in Chile it was 40; and in South Africa it was 33.[19] 'Globalisation' is not a convincing excuse for inequality. Global equalisation requires that the popular, disadvantaged forces of the inegalitarian countries are strengthened.

There are mechanisms of equality - already tried and tested - as well as mechanisms of inequality. Thus rapprochement is the opposite of distantiation, whether this is achieved through catching up or by compensating for handicaps. China and India are catching up after regaining their national sovereignty around 1950 - arguably a more significant break with the past than the turn to state-guided capitalism in China from 1978 and to capitalist liberalisation in India from around 1990. Within countries, affirmative action in favour of scheduled castes and tribes in India, in favour of women from South Asia to the North Atlantic, and in favour of African-Americans in the US, have been significant in reducing inequalities.

Inclusion (as opposed to exclusion) has brought women into public space and labour markets in many parts of the globe. Recently it has changed the Creole coloniality of some of the Amerindian republics of Latin America, especially in Bolivia and Ecuador, though defeats have been suffered in Guatemala, Peru and elsewhere. But the issue of how to include the 'First Nations' into the polity of the twenty-first century remains on the agenda, from Chile to Canada. The European Union has also made a contribution recently, through the inclusion of an impoverished Eastern Europe into its area of prosperity.

In retrospect, the managerial moves away from hierarchy that began in the 1980s turn out to have led, in terms of income, to the vanishing of the middle, with a greater polarisation between top and bottom, rather than to have been a measure of equalisation. Gains from post-hierarchical informalisation can perhaps be expected, but hard evidence seems to be unavailable.

Redistribution and recompensation are also powerful tools for addressing inequality. Denmark and Sweden are the least income unequal countries of the world.[20] The Danish welfare state spends 28 per cent of GDP on social expenditure, the Swedish 31 per cent - while the UK spends 20 per cent.[21] Yet both Denmark and Sweden are heavily dependent on the world market: merchandise export makes up 35 per cent of Danish Gross National Income and 40 per cent of Swedish - compared to 17 per cent in the UK. Pro-marketeers will perhaps ask whether this equality and generosity is sustainable in the context of the world market. The irrefutable answer is yes. For many years the Scandinavian countries have scored well on competitiveness as well as on equality. They consistently appear at the top in the Davos World Economic Forum *Global Competitiveness Reports* (together with the USA and Switzerland). In the 2006-2008 editions, Denmark was ranked at no 3 in global competitiveness, and in 2007-8 Sweden was no 4, while New Labour Britain was at no 9, down from no 2 in 2006-7.[22]

While these composite rankings should always be taken with a pinch of salt by serious observers, the recurrent success of the Nordic welfare states on a world capitalist list (with Finland on rung 6 and oil-rich Norway on 16 among 131 countries) certainly means that generous, relatively egalitarian welfare states should not be seen as utopias or protected enclaves, but as highly competitive participants in the world market. In other words, even within the parameters of global capitalism there are many degrees of freedom for radical social alternatives. And the literally lethal effects of inequality make searching for them imperative.

Notes

1. Calculated from R. Fitzpatrick and T. Charandola, 'Health', in A.H. Halsey and J. Webb (eds), *Twentieth-Century British Social Trends*, Macmillan 2000, table 3.8.

2. M. Marmot, *The Status Syndrome*, Bloomsbury 2004.

3. A. Maddison, *Contours of the World Economy, 1-2030 AD*, Oxford University Press 2007, table A5.

4. UNDP, *Human Development Report 2007/8*, Geneva 2007, table 10.

5. A joint Bristol and Sheffield University study, reported on the BBC News 29.4.2005.

6. WHO Commission on Social Determinants of Health, *Closing the Gap in a*

Generation, WHO 2008, table 2.1; M. Marmot, 'Social determinants of health inequalities', *Lancet*, Vol. 365, issue 9464, pp1099-1104.

7. UNDP 2007, op cit, table 10.

8. Maddison, op cit, table A5; UNDP 2007, op cit, table 14.

9. T. Piketty, 'Top Incomes Over the Twentieth Century: A Summary of Main Findings', in A.B. Atkinson and T. Piketty (eds), *Top Incomes over the Twentieth Century*, Oxford University Press 2007, p12.

10. Office for National Statistics, *Survey of Personal Incomes 2006-07*, updated in December 2008, table 3.1.

11. Historical data from Maddison, op cit, table 5.9b; executive pay, IDS *Directors' Pay Report 2008*, www.incomesdata.co.uk; median earnings from ONS, C. Dobbs, *Patterns of pay: results of the Annual Survey of Hours and Earnings 1997 to 2008*. In fairness, it should be added that in 1688 the very top, the temporal lords, appropriated 400 times higher income than labourers.

12. www.forbes.com/forbes/2009, accessed 12.3.2009.

13. Marmott 2004, op cit, p196.

14. Department for Work and Pensions, *Households Below Average Income report*, release, 7 May 2009.

15. Atkinson and Piketty, op cit.

16. G. Tett, 'Lost through destructive creation', *Financial Times*, 10.3.09, p11.

17. UNDP 2007, op cit, table 28.

18. OECD, *Growing Unequal?*, OECD 2008, p37.

19. B. Milanovic, 'Even higher inequality than previously thought: a note on global inequality calculations using the 2005 international comparison program results', *International Journal of Health Services*, Vol. 38: 3 2008, table 2; UNDP 2007, op cit, table 15.

20. OECD 2008, op cit, p52.

21 OECD, *Society at a Glance*, OECD 2007.

22. K. Schwab and M. Porter, *The Global Competiveness Report 2007-2008*, World Economic Forum 2007, table 4.

The living wage

Jane Wills

In spite of the minimum wage, many low-paid workers continue to struggle to fund the necessities of life.

———

At a time when economic crisis is prompting activists to look for new ideas about the way ahead, it is useful to look back to the lessons of history. Here I explore contemporary efforts to popularise the idea of a living wage, contrasting the campaigns which flourished between the 1870s and 1920s with more recent demands. In both periods, work has been associated with 'sweating' - characterised by low pay, long hours and poor conditions - often in relations of subcontracted employment. This time round, however, the demand for a living wage is being made in countries as diverse as America, Bangladesh, Britain and Sri Lanka. The demand for a living wage is travelling along the sinews of the sub-contracted global economy, as workers seek to challenge the 'real employers' at the top of contracting chains. My argument is that the demand for a living wage can provide the means to challenge the very structure of this subcontracted economy, and to secure greater justice for those doing the work.

The first living wage campaign

The notion of a living wage first emerged in the industrial heartlands of Britain during the 1870s, as the burgeoning labour movement developed the capacity to bargain over their share of economic pie. As Sidney and Beatrice Webb argued, the early trade unions started to challenge the 'doctrine of supply and demand' with the 'doctrine of a living wage'.[1] Workers began to demand the wages that would allow them to buy the food, shelter and clothing needed for themselves and their families to live. Rather than accepting that wages would be set by the vagaries of the market - the laws of supply and demand - workers were agitating for minimum standards that would allow them the means to survive.

The first full-length treatise in defence of a living wage - as far as I have been able to discover - was written in 1894 by Mark Oldroyd, when he was Liberal MP for Dewsbury, Yorkshire. Oldroyd had a textile factory employing 2500 people in the town, and from our perspective - living as we do in an age of irresponsible capitalism - it can only seem remarkable that when invited to give a lecture to the Dewsbury Pioneers Industrial Society (later the Dewsbury Co-operative Society) in December 1894, he chose the topic of the living wage. As many as one hundred and fourteen years ago, a liberal industrialist - who was also a passionate non-conformist Christian - declared: 'A living wage must be sufficient to maintain the worker in the highest state of industrial efficiency, with decent surroundings and sufficient leisure'.[2]

Oldroyd declared that the living wage should provide the basic subsistence needed by a worker and his family (as would be expected, the language and arguments reflect the gender norms of the time); it should provide 'reasonable time for recreation and rest' as well as 'reasonable home comforts'; and be sufficient to allow him to 'discharge ... the duties of citizenship'. The living wage was to be paid for by increased efficiency; greater consumption, which would help fuel demand; and in some cases by falling profits and/or rising prices. But Oldroyd's argument was ethical as well as economic: the living wage was seen as a way to recognise the 'moral worth' of labour itself. Workers were to be afforded the dignity of providing for themselves by dint of their work.

At this time, many in the growing labour movement were particularly exercised by the effects of sweating, whereby workers were exploited beyond their capacity to recuperate. Even after long hours of arduous work they were paid less than they needed to reproduce themselves and their families. In response, political activists and social reformers began to advocate minimum standards for education, sanitation, leisure and wages, including a 'National Minimum' wage. These arguments prompted the government to pass the Trade Boards Act of 1909, setting new standards in a number of low-waged industries, including chain making and lace finishing, which involved many women working at home, as well as wholesale tailoring and paper-box making, where margins were low and sweating was common. In what were to become the Wages Councils after the second world war, these boards involved employers, worker representatives and independent assessors in setting minimum standards for wages, hours and conditions of work.

At the same time, social reformers sought to calculate the real living wage. In the early years of the twentieth century, another industrialist, Benjamin Seebohm Rowntree, son of Joseph Rowntree, Quaker, philanthropist and chocolate manufacturer, developed the tool kit for calculating the living wage, or what he called 'the human costs of labour'. Rowntree did meticulous research in York to price the food, rent, clothing, fuel and miscellaneous items needed by a man with three children. He then advocated the extension of Trade Boards to cover each industry; these would fix wages around the new standard (35 shillings and 3 pence a week at 1914 prices for all adult men), while overseeing the industrial reforms needed to increase productivity and cover the cost. Rowntree argued that the nation depended on a living wage to ensure its workers were fit and healthy enough to work and take part in the wider community.

The demand for a living wage was then taken up as official policy by the Independent Labour Party from 1925. A living wage bill was proposed in the House of Commons in February 1931 by James Maxton MP (the subject of a biography by none other than Gordon Brown MP), and - with remarkable contemporary resonance - Maxton located the policy within the context of the curse of under-consumption. At a time of economic crisis and high unemployment, and in the wake of the general strike, Maxton and his ILP colleagues sought to focus on the politics of consumption as well as production. A living wage, they argued, would allow the population to consume 'the essential things of life ... food, better housing accommodation, better furnishing, equipment inside their home, better illumination of those homes, and better sanitation'.[3] This, in turn, would stimulate growth, jobs and prosperity for the nation at large: putting money into the pockets of poor people was argued to be a way out of decline. In the event, though 124 Labour party MPs voted in support of the Bill, it failed to win sufficient support, and the notion of a living wage was not to resurface as a political demand in Britain until the recent call and campaign led by London Citizens since 2001.

Whatever happened to the living wage?

With hindsight, it is clear that during the post-war years the welfare state gradually eclipsed the demand for a living wage. The provision of education, health, housing and pensions - together with the growth of collective bargaining and the operation of Wages Councils - relegated to the sidelines the demand for a living wage. During the twentieth century, the state tended to lay down minimum standards for pay - which have generally been less than subsistence standards - and then provided a 'top-up' depending on need and political pressure. However, by the 1970s poverty was creeping back into everyday life. In particular, those workers who had not collectivised their wage setting, and were left to the Wages Councils, had seen a relative decline in their levels of pay. Wages Councils still covered as many 3.5 million workers by the late 1970s, and most had minimum standards little better than benefit levels.

These workers stood little chance of withstanding the whirlwind of market forces that were unleashed by Mrs Thatcher's Conservative governments during the 1980s. These governments introduced market testing to the NHS and compulsory competitive tendering to local government, and enacted widespread privatisation. The market was treated as a public good. Any obstacles to the operation of market forces were opposed, and trade union reforms were accompanied by the abolition of Fair Wages in contracting in 1983, and of the Wages Councils in 1993. Wages were once more being increasingly determined by the laws of supply and demand. As was inevitable, inequality grew. Between 1977 and 1991, the share of total disposable income received by the top 20 per cent of households increased from 36 to 42 per cent. The share received by those in the lowest 60 per cent fell, while the share of the bottom 20 per cent fell from 10 to 7 per cent.[4]

The model of capitalism that emerged from this period is now widely known as neoliberalism, and its preferred form of employment relationship has been subcontracting, which is now common across the public and private sectors in all parts of the world. Large multinational corporations have been able to source their goods - and, increasingly, their services - from suppliers in a growing diversity of nations, getting them to tender for work and thus reduce costs. Furthermore, as economic activity and market relations have taken hold in poorer parts of the world, rates of international migration have also increased. As Douglas Massey and colleagues put it in their overview of scholarship in the field: 'International migration does not stem from a lack of economic development, but from development itself'.[5] Processes of economic globalisation have extended local markets and the desire for material goods, along with the money and physical infrastructure needed to move;

and they have also played a major role in generating the widening inequalities and impoverishment that have further encouraged international migration. Increasing numbers of people from the Global South and East have found their way North and West, and Britain has become a nation of immigration rather than emigration during the past twenty years. Many such migrants have acted as Marx said they would: they have become a reserve army of labour, taking up degraded employment in more affluent countries. Recent research into London's low-paid economy has exposed the extent to which our city now depends on these migrant labour supplies; in what we have called London's Migrant Division of Labour, a number of us working together at Queen Mary have highlighted the extent to which sectors such as care, cleaning, construction and hospitality are now dependent upon foreign-born staff.[6]

In this context, it should be no surprise that the demand for a living wage has resurfaced in the early years of our new century. In London, the low-paid labour market is characterised by subcontracted employment, and this has a deflationary impact on the terms and conditions of work. People have to work long hours in low paid jobs in order to survive. In addition, even if they have tried, trade unions have struggled to organise amongst these workers, and have largely failed to improve the terms of the work. However, while the living wage was championed as a means to secure the well-being of the nation between the 1870s and the 1920s, today's call for a living wage echoes far beyond the shores of the United Kingdom. On the one hand, the earning levels of migrants in countries like the UK impact on the money sent home in remittances - which now exceeds that awarded in international aid.[7] On the other hand, the demand for a living wage can also be extended to cover all those labouring to make the goods that we buy. For these reasons the demand for a living wage has been taken up by the movement for Corporate Social Responsibility and bodies such as the Ethical Trading Initiative, to try to ensure some measure of justice for workers abroad. Indeed, the campaign against sweatshops abroad has often been more vigorous than that conducted against the practice of sweating at home.

Beyond the National Minimum Wage

When they came into power in 1997 New Labour recognised the need to tackle low pay. The 1998 National Minimum Wage Act provided for the establishment of a Low Pay Commission, which now sets Britain's National Minimum Wage (NMW). The first rate, set in April 1999, was £3.60 an hour for adults aged over 22, and covered as many as 1.2 million adults, who had an average pay rise of 10 per cent. There is evidence that the NMW has reversed half the increase in inequality of the Thatcher era without any detrimental impact on employment; and there is some evidence that it has been responsible for greater productivity, some reductions in hours, some price increases and some falls in profits.[8] Compliance appears to have been remarkably high, and in tandem with working tax credit and child tax credit, the NMW has set new income standards for Britain. But while the NMW has clearly had a very positive impact on the incidence of low pay and income inequality, this approach has a number of limits, and there is a need to go beyond this. Outlined below are five limitations of the NMW that are particularly pertinent in the context of the subcontracted economy.

Firstly, the NMW has been set at a level determined by the market rather than Seebohm Rowntree's concept of the 'human needs of labour'. Section 7 of the 1998 Act requires that the Low Pay Commission consult employers' and workers' representative bodies in making their recommendations, and in so doing: 'have regard to the effect of this Act on the economy of the United Kingdom as a whole and on competitiveness'. The wage reflects what the market will bear rather than what is actually required to live. At its present level of £5.73 an hour, a worker earns £230 for a 40-hour week (just under £12,000 a year) before stoppages. Recent research funded by the Joseph Rowntree Foundation has confirmed that in the UK even a single person with no dependents, living in council housing, needs £13,400 a year before tax to afford a basic but acceptable standard of living. This sum translates as £6.88 an hour, well above the NMW. London's own living wage rate is currently £7.60 an hour - approximately £15,000 a year before stoppages; but even this is calculated on the basis of full benefit take up. Without means-tested benefits the London living wage needs to be as much as £9.85 an hour.[9]

Many workers in London earn well below the living wage rate. The Greater London Authority puts the figure at about 1 in 5, or 400,000 people. Many of these workers have dependents to support, and they often are the only working adult in the family. As already indicated, the majority of them are migrants to the UK, and many do not have access to the benefit system. They include international students, new arrivals from central and eastern Europe and irregular migrants who

The living wage

are not eligible to claim the in-work benefits that are available to their colleagues. Even if they were paid the London living wage - which would represent a 40 per cent pay rise from the NMW - these workers would still not be earning enough money, because of this lack of support. As a result many work long hours, take up second or third jobs and share their accommodation with others. I will never forget interviewing one woman from the Caribbean who cleaned at Canary Wharf from 9pm at night, then cleaned a hospital every morning and then managed to look after some elderly people in the evening before returning to Canary Wharf to clean. This woman had a herculean appetite for work, sleeping only at the weekend and always falling asleep on the tube going home. She had a young son at home, and had had a stroke during the previous year. Many other workers we have spoken to are similarly overstretched, studying during the day and working at night. The NMW is not sufficient to keep workers out of poverty, particularly if they have no access to the benefit system.

The second argument against the current system is that it involves a huge subsidy to very wealthy employers. While subcontracting - and the attendant competition for contracts - has kept margins and wages low for key services and workers alike, it is the clients of the subcontractors who have really benefited. It is easy to blame the contractors, but many of them are themselves forced into a downward spiral of competition for tenders that makes it impossible to offer better wages even if they wanted to. In contrast, large private companies - some of them posting eye-watering profits - have saved money by subcontracting their catering, cleaning and security operations and/or by sourcing their goods from suppliers abroad. Low-paid workers have been sweated in the interests of these companies, and where they have been eligible the state has assisted by topping up their pay to reflect their real needs: tax credits cost as much as £20 billion in 2007/8. This is all the more galling in that - while low-paid workers and tax-payers are subsidising them - these same corporations are avoiding their tax liabilities. The National Audit Office has indicated that in 2006 more than 60 per cent of Britain's 700 biggest companies paid less than £10m corporation tax, and 30 per cent paid nothing. The TUC have estimated that the 'tax gap' is as high as £12bn - equivalent to around 480 new schools, 300 hospitals or more than 1.3m new nursery places.[10]

In addition, the Migrant Division of Labour means that the clients of the subcontractors are also subsidised by foreign nations. The Ghanaian and Polish governments - to take an example of two countries whose workers feature heavily among low-paid migrants - have funded their education and health systems, however marginally, only to see their best and brightest depart. Doreen Massey has written powerfully about the way in which London is made through its relationships to the rest of the world; and the exploitation of cheap foreign labour - in situ or in London - is a critical part of this process.[11] As she suggests, the wealth of our city depends on its geographical relationships with the rest of the world. Paying a living wage would begin to address some of the responsibilities that should come with our wealth, not least because some of the money would be remitted back home.

A third criticism of the subcontracting system and its reliance on cheap labour is the effect it has in the public sector. The subcontracting practices deployed there to save money simultaneously contradict the core aims of the bodies involved. The public sector is designed to improve the collective good in some way - to improve the health of the nation, to foster community cohesion, to educate future generations - and yet, by supporting employment systems that perpetuate low pay and poor conditions of work, these organisations are creating many of the problems they purport to prevent. In our research we have interviewed hospital cleaners who don't get sick pay and go to work when they are sick; we have met people who have young children at home and yet work two jobs in care and hospital cleaning so they can put food on the table, thus missing out on homework and life after school; and we have spoken to carers who are working long hours looking after other people's families while neglecting their own. Just as in the 1890s, the low-paid economy has costs for the wider community. Improving the quality of low-paid employment - and efforts to tackle the effects of subcontracting in particular - would contribute to the core goals of social inclusion, ending child poverty and re-skilling the nation. It is impossible to overstate how important this is. Recent months have seen the violent deaths of more than twenty young people in London, and it is no coincidence that these crimes take place in the poorest and most excluded communities. Respecting and rewarding low-paid workers would have dramatic knock-on effects in our poorest communities. Experience at Queen Mary suggests that it would also improve the quality of the work that is done.[12]

This relates to a fourth issue - which is probably the most important matter of all. The combination of subcontracting and state intervention to set minimum standards makes it much easier for employers to avoid their moral responsibility for the conditions of work. Subcontracting means that many large private and public bodies have no relationship with the people on whom they depend. In contrast with Mark Oldroyd or the Rowntrees, our business leaders and public officials appear to feel no responsibility for the people doing their work. The absence of an employment contract severs any moral contract between 'real employers' and workers. The workers might be down the corridor cleaning the loo or they might be thousands of miles away at the end of a complex supply chain sewing jeans in a factory in a free trade zone, but they no longer feature in the consciousness of the people that benefit from their work. As London Citizens found in the early days of the living wage campaign in London, most 'real employers' are happy to leave their staff to the contractor and the laws of the market.

This divorce between those who generate wealth and those who accumulate it is a critical factor in the moral malaise in our society today. A freedom of information enquiry by the *Evening Standard* during 2007 revealed that only 65 of the 400-odd people thought to 'earn' at least £10 million a year declared their income for the purpose of tax. Many of the richest people in Britain now pay less tax than the cleaners whom they choose to ignore. They are able to justify this, in part, because they have no connection to the people they really employ and the society in which the rest of us live.

This abdication of responsibility is further reinforced by our collective view of the state. Since the early years of the twentieth century, progressives have tended to make demands on the state. Led by the Fabians, people have assumed that our problems can be dealt with by some part of the government's machinery. But even if this were true, this mindset has devastating psychological consequences. It allows us to avoid our responsibility for the systems of which we are part. Many of our lowest paid workers are neglected just because no-one thinks about them and their conditions of work. In our everyday lives, we all take the labour of poor workers for granted. The demand for a living wage asks the real employers to take responsibility for the people doing their work, and it calls upon all of us to reflect on the prices of the consumer goods and services that we buy, as well as the wages of the people cleaning our workplace.

The fifth key problem arising from the prevalence of subcontracted capitalism is that it means that the people who have a direct interest in challenging low pay have little power to change it. Between 2005 and 2007 we interviewed more than 400 migrant workers in low paid employment in London and found that while almost all were receiving the NMW (bar some hospitality workers who were paid to clean by the room), only 7 per cent were paid the living wage or above. Most had just 20 days paid holiday (including 8 bank holidays), very few had access to occupational sick pay or a pension, and only a quarter reported having an annual pay rise.[13] These workers were 'sweated': they worked hard for wages that did not allow them the minimum standards needed to live. Yet while subcontracting, low pay and poor conditions of work provide reasons to organise, they also make it much harder to win battles. In relationships of subcontracted capitalism, those with the real power over the contracting process - the ultimate employers of all those involved in any particular supply chain or business operation - are generally not accessible to those doing the work. Meaningful collective bargaining is impossible. Even if workers did get organised, join a union and improve their terms and conditions of work, they would in all likelihood price themselves out of a job. To effectively recalibrate the terms and conditions of employment requires that workers get to the 'real employers' at the top of contracting chains.[14]

It is not only migrant workers who suffer in this system. Linda McDowell has written movingly about the young men who leave school without qualifications and find they have to grapple with the low-paid subcontracted service economy to find their way in the world.[15] Our society now offers little to young people who aren't able or willing to stay on in education. There is little opportunity or respect for the people who have to try to make a living from manual work. Any effort to make bad jobs better would help this group, just as it might be a better way to entice the unemployed back into work than cutting benefits. It would clearly also help those migrants already doing the jobs, even if it slowed down demand for such migrant labour in future. The demand for a living wage thus makes it possible to construct a broad coalition to secure such reform, trying to enforce responsibility on those employers who are more than able to pay.

What is being done?

London Citizens - a broad-based alliance of faith, labour and educational organisations - launched a living wage campaign in April 2001. This arose partly through the experience of sister organisations across the Atlantic - notably in

The living wage

Baltimore - where the living wage movement took off during the mid-1990s, but it also arose from the very structure of London's economy. Member organisations of London Citizens - many of them populated by the migrant communities on which London has come to rely - raised the issues of low pay and subcontracting as their major concerns. Their members had no time to volunteer, no time for family life, and were ground down by the very nature of work.

Just like Seebohm Rowntree almost a hundred years ago, the campaign began by calculating a new living wage. Once this was done, the campaign sought to target the 'real employers' who could or should pay: the accountants, banks, consultants, legal organisations, hospitals, hotels, universities, charities and art galleries. London Citizens' alliance of more than one hundred different groups - including my own university department - worked together to try to mobilise workers within any contracted labour force alongside their allies in the community to demand improvements in the terms and conditions of work. To date, the campaign has secured living wage agreements that cover almost 6000 workers, redistributing millions of pounds to the poor.

More than just targeting particular employers, however - and the latest targets are universities and luxury hotels in the build-up to the Olympics in 2012 - this campaign has also been part of a wider effort to remake the city itself. London Citizens seeks to empower poor communities and teach active citizenship through political campaigns. While low-wage workers are part of this movement - and some branches of the trade unions UNISON and Unite (T&G) have been actively involved through the living wage campaign - they are not left to do battle alone. The coalition has effectively allowed the 'scaling-up' of workers' issues to the level of the wider community. The institutional infrastructure of organisations such as the Roman Catholic Church, the intellectual resources of universities, and the political machinery of London's government have been mobilised in pursuit of a living wage, along with demands for the regularisation of migrants, social housing and community safety. The alliance has generated sufficient power to call London's business leaders and politicians to account for the state of the city at large.

There are strong historical echoes to this latest campaign. The first wave of agitation for a living wage was the cry of an emergent social movement. The demand for a living wage involved a coalition of voices including trade unionists, political activists, faith leaders and intellectuals. While demands were made for a just wage, activists used a variety of different mechanisms to secure this goal. The trade unions sought to bargain for better wages; social reformers like Booth and Rowntree provided the research material; the Webbs and others advocated government action to pay a National Minimum; and yet others exercised their political power to ensure that fair wages were paid. As early as 1889 this movement had sufficient political muscle to ensure that the London School Board, Nottingham Corporation and London County Council had adopted fair wages clauses in their contracting procedures. Tower Hamlets Liberal MP Sydney Buxton introduced a similar proposal in the House of Commons in 1891, and as many as 48 county boroughs, 54 non-county boroughs and 116 other urban districts enacted fair wages clauses in their contracts by 1898.[16] The emergent labour movement was able to use its rising economic and political power to secure increases in pay.

A victim of its own success, and in the face of intense economic restructuring and the anti-union laws of the 1980s, this broad church of the socialist and labour movement gradually disintegrated during the latter years of the twentieth century. As is well documented, the Labour Party became New Labour, and the trade unions became increasingly focused on the interests of their members rather than the wider community of which they were part. The faith groups were victims of secularisation, and the academics stopped raising their voice. As a result, poor workers without collective organisation have tended to remain poor, and those without collective muscle have tended to remain powerless. Jobs such as cleaning and hospitality - long carried out by women and now often filled by migrants - were simply neglected. London Citizens has been filling a vacuum left by the left, and the living wage campaign has facilitated the alliance building needed to effect social change.

Against all the odds, London Citizens has proved that it is possible to tackle the subcontracted low wage economy and its political consequences. The campaign has fostered solidarity across incredible diversity, including class, faith, culture and generation, and in so doing it has raised the spectre of a different kind of moral economy. I end with the words of Professor Leonard Trelawny Hobhouse, the first British Professor of Sociology, appointed to a chair at the LSE in 1907. Here he is speaking about the living wage at the Inter-Dominational Summer School, Swanwick, Derbyshire, in the summer of 1913. His words resonate strongly with our situation today. History tells us that there is great scope in agitating for a living wage during a time of recession, seeking to reward the poor as a route to recovery.

The living wage

As Hobhouse declared:

> A society in which a large proportion of honest and industrious workers are unable to secure continuous employment at a wage which will maintain a family in a condition compatible with the requirements of physical health is fundamentally an ill-organised society; it has failed to secure a primary condition of healthy social life, and a society which sits down passively under such conditions and lets them alone is not only an ill-organised society but one which has lost faith in itself or is dead to its responsibilities. Hence it is that the problem of the living wage lies at the foundation of social life.[17]

———

Notes

1. S. and B. Webb, *Industrial Democracy*, Longmans, Green and Co (1911)[1897].

2. M. Oldroyd, *A Living Wage*, McCorquodale and Co Ltd 1894.

3. J. Maxton, *A living wage for all*, speech moving the second reading of the living wage bill, 6 February 1931, ILP Publications 1931.

4. ONS Data on inequality, 2008, from www.statistics.gov.uk (last accessed February 2009).

5. D. Massey, J. Arango, G. Hugo, A. Kouaouci, A. Pellegrino and J. Taylor, *Worlds in Motion: understanding international migration at the end of the millennium*, Clarendon Press 1998.

6. See J. May, J. Wills, K. Datta, Y. Evans, J. Herbert and C. McIlwaine, 'Keeping London working: Global cities, the British state, and London's new migrant division of labour', *Transactions of the Institute of British Geographers* 32, 2, 2007; J. Wills, K. Datta, Y. Evans, J. Herbert, J. May and C. McIlwaine, 'London's migrant division of labour', *European Journal of Urban and Regional Studies* (2009 forthcoming); and J. Wills, K. Datta, Y. Evans, J. Herbert, J. May and C. McIlwaine, *Global cities at work: New migrant divisions of labour*, Pluto Press 2009.

7. K. Datta, C. McIlwaine, J. Wills, Y. Evans, J. Herbert and J. May, 'The new development finance or exploiting migrant labour? Remittance sending among low-paid migrant workers in London', *International Development Planning Review*, 29, 1, 2007.

8. D. Metcalf, *Why has the British National Minimum Wage had little or no impact on employment?* CEP Discussion Paper 781, 2007.

9. Greater London Authority, *A fairer London: The 2009 living wage in London*, GLA 2009.

10. 'Firms' secret tax avoidance schemes cost UK billions: Investigation into the complex and confidential world of tax', *Guardian*, 2.2.09; www.guardian. co.uk/business/2009/feb/02/tax-gap-avoidance.

11. D. Massey, *World City*, Polity Press 2007.

12. J. Wills, with N. Kakpo and R. Begum, *The Business Case for the Living Wage: the story of the cleaning service at Queen Mary*, Queen Mary, University of London, 2009; available from www.geog.qmul.ac.uk/staff/willsj.html.

13. *Global Cities at Work* (see note 6).

14. J.Wills, 'Subcontracted employment and its challenge to labor', *Labor Studies Journal* (2009 forthcoming).

15. L. McDowell, *Redundant Masculinities: Employment change and white working class youth*, Blackwell 2003.

16. B. Bercusson, *Fair wages resolutions*, Studies in Labour and Social Law Volume 2, Mansell 1978.

17. L. T. Hobhouse, 'The right to a living wage', in *The industrial unrest and the living wage: Lectures given at the interdenominational Summer School, held at Swanwick, Derbyshire, June 28th to July 5th 1913*, 1913.

Academies: privatising England's schools

Terry Wrigley

Privatising schools will not solve England's educational problems.

———

L ord Harris informed the *Financial Times* in June 2007: 'I have a very good relationship with Andrew [Lord Adonis, then Schools Minister]. He rings me up and says, "Do you want this school?" and I ask what it's like and if it sounds like the sort of place that we are interested in I say yes.'

This quotation neatly illustrates the subjectivity and arbitrariness that is involved in the transformation of schools into academies - in effect the transference of power from locally elected bodies to business leaders. However it is not simply the initial establishment of academies that is at stake in this process, but the power relationships under which they are subsequently controlled. As lawyers have pointed out, once a school becomes an academy, education law, which regulates state schools and provides important protection to parents, students and staff, is discarded. The sponsor has almost absolute power: appointing the headteacher and (after initial transfers) other staff; and determining who will be on its board of governors, the nature of the curriculum, the design of any new buildings, and which young people to include or exclude. As many parents of children with special educational needs have discovered, it is no use lobbying your councillor if provision for your child is inadequate.

Government ministers deny that academies are a form of privatisation (despite

David Blunkett's initial bluntness on first announcing that they would be '*owned and run* by sponsors'). But the government defence depends on a narrow interpretation of privatisation: it argues that academies are not for profit (well, not yet); that they are funded from the public purse (but then so is the arms industry); and that they are subject to some rules regarding admissions - a concession resulting from a back bench revolt (but then all private businesses face some legal restrictions). Academies are clearly privatised bodies on any broader definition, since they are institutions that have been withdrawn from collective democratic accountability and delivered over into the power of individuals and unaccountable institutions. In all important respects, power over children's education is being handed over to a rag-tag bunch of second-hand car dealers, carpet salesmen and tax-evading city traders.

The first stage of this handover has not gone well for the government. In the absence of cutting-edge high-tech companies rushing forward to replace local authorities in the running of schools, the government was forced into what is in effect a re-launching of the process, with universities and evangelical fractions of the Church of England becoming the sponsors of choice. This has only led to new problems. Universities have been chosen as sponsors that don't even have teacher education departments, and some prestigious institutions such as Cambridge University and the Institute of Education in London have refused to participate. Principled opposition has come from the Universities and Colleges Union (UCU), and local campaign groups opposing academies have continued to grow.

Paradoxically, a few local authorities have now been accepted as sponsors - partly as a result of the government's desperation, but also as an effect of the complex hybridisation of public and private as neoliberalism continues to evolve. Within a week of hearing from a Director of Education that local councillors had outwitted the government by offering that the authority should become co-sponsors of some academies, I was emailed by a company boasting that they were installing a practice call-centre into one of those schools - 'to raise aspirations' (sic).

Similarly, Manchester's plan to co-sponsor six of its own schools as academies is tied to the vocationalising of school learning: 10-year-old children and their parents are expected to choose secondary schools on the basis of career interests. I can imagine the conversation: 'Please can I go to the Manchester Airport Academy of Travel and Tourism mummy, so that I can become a baggage handler when I grow up'.

The privatisation process has been gathering pace over the past two decades,

Academies: privatising England's schools

across basic public services such as schools, hospitals and council housing. In education it began in the mid 1980s, when school meals provision and cleaning were put out to tender. (Predictably, local healthy eating initiatives went out the window.) It then spread to support services such as careers advice and staff development, before reaching a high point when private businesses were handed not only the construction projects for new schools but also the ownership and control of the buildings themselves, under the Private Finance Initiative (PFI, later PPP and Building Schools for the Future). These have provided a real bonanza for construction firms and banks, who now own school buildings and land, and rent them out to the education authorities.

However the academies mark a qualitative change in this expanding involvement of the private sector, since they involve transferring control of the education process itself into private hands (the curriculum, teaching, school relationships). Nor is this a marginal project: the government's declared intention is that academies (still mostly urban and secondary) should be followed by Trust Schools (which can be secondary, primary or special, and in any location).

What is ultimately at stake is the changing purpose of education. As Stephen Ball argues in *The Education Debate* (2008, pp11-12):

> Within policy, education is now regarded primarily from an economic point of view. The social and economic purposes of education have been collapsed into a single, overriding emphasis on policy making for economic competitiveness and an increasing neglect or sidelining (other than in rhetoric) of the social purposes of education.

Ball describes in great detail, in this and his previous book *Education PLC* (2007), the extent to which education policy has become dominated by issues of economic competitiveness within a global economy which is understood in neoliberal terms.

Perhaps the biggest marker of this changing emphasis in English school policy is the clause in the 2006 education act which divides the school population into two from age 14 onwards - an academic and a vocational track. The former will be entitled to a broad and balanced curriculum, including English, maths, science, a foreign language, history or geography, a design and technology subject, and one of the arts (including media). The latter, pursuing a work-related diploma, will receive a narrower and more functionalist version of the 'core' (English, maths and science) and have no entitlement to a foreign language, history or geography, design and technology, or the arts. This is both a deep incursion into the comprehensive school principle, and a shift in educational purpose such that preparation for work would dominate. (It is important to emphasise that I am not arguing here against vocational subjects, but against them dominating the curriculum and dividing students into two halves.)

There is always the possibility lurking that the academies project is intended to pave the way for private companies to make a profit out of state-funded schools, as is already happening with many US Charter Schools and a few Swedish schools. At present, though, the greater threat is posed by this new structure of privatised management, directed by a unit of the DCSF, which appears dedicated to the most rapid possible reorientation towards a narrower educational purpose. Almost all academies have a business or related specialism. In many, history, geography and the arts have essentially been sacrificed to new vocational qualifications. Overwhelmingly, academies are using their autonomy to convert the curriculum into preparation for work - often for insecure low-paid jobs - to the neglect of other educational aims such as personal expression through the arts and a critical understanding of social and environmental issues.

The impact of private governance

There is no space here to examine all the ramifications of private control. Already some excellent resources are available. These include Francis Beckett's book *The Great City Academy Fraud* (2007); a special issue of Forum *The academy fiasco* (2008); and the findings of a Commons enquiry involving presentations from many local campaign groups (*Report on the MPs Committee of enquiry into academies and trust schools*, 12 June 2007). All these, and other substantial information, can be found on the website of the Anti-Academies Alliance (www.antiacademies.org.uk). My aim here is to provide a few headlines from these various sources.

One of the main problems in academies is the arbitrariness of forms of control. Most state schools already enjoy substantial autonomy. The majority of their governing body consists of elected representatives of parents and staff. In the academies, however, the board is appointed by the sponsor, who even decides who will represent the staff. The sponsor also chooses the head, and the rest of the staff, as well as deciding on their pay and conditions. Despite the legal safeguards for staff from the predecessor school, conflict is already occurring as sponsors deny rights of trade union representation and attempts are made to lengthen working hours; not surprisingly, many academies suffer from high levels of staff turnover and inexperienced teachers.

In some instances the religious convictions of sponsors appear to override other considerations, as in the following witness statement from a local campaign group to the MPs enquiry:

> Instead of being asked about teaching style he was quizzed on his views on birth control and whether or not he believed in Noah's Ark … 'I was cut short by a sarcastic and disturbing comment - What's the point of sending young people out into the world with 20 GCSEs when they're going to Hell?' [The interviewee complaining about this treatment was not anti-religious: he was himself a Methodist lay preacher!]

In some cases, the religious fervour of academy sponsors has led to disciplinary regimes worthy of a boot camp.

The greatest incentive to winning consent for a change to academy status is the promise of an impressive new building. The additional cost of such buildings vastly outweighs the sponsor's £2,000,000 contribution (which is any case often fictitious). And in spite of the fact that almost all the cost of the new buildings comes from the public purse, many of them become monuments to the sponsor's ego. Many academies look impressive but cold: shiny steel and glass surfaces, grey and brown colour schemes, and balconies and spaces designed for surveillance, with few quiet places to sit, relax and work collaboratively - other than at computers. They often appear to be modelled on City offices, rather than seeking to provide a welcoming social and learning environment for inner-city adolescents. The Bexley Business Academy has had to be substantially rebuilt: classrooms had been designed without a fourth wall. In one case a nearly new sports hall was demolished and rebuilt, at a cost of £1,000,000, to avoid paying VAT when the building was hired out for community use. A Peterborough academy was built without a playground or recreational space. When reporters challenged the head on this he replied that the students wouldn't need such space because they wouldn't have any free time either

- but they would be able to drink water during lessons. Actually, his precise words were: 'They will be able to hydrate during the learning experience'.

The ethics of buying control of a school are dubious. And scandals soon emerged, such as the sponsorship moneys that went unpaid, the special offer to 'sponsor three for the price of two', instances of money finding its way back to the sponsors or their relatives, and the discovery that some potential sponsors were being bribed with the offer of peerages.

Sponsors clearly have a variety of motives, from religious zeal and public esteem to a more general desire to make education more business-oriented. Some have used the rhetoric of philanthropy - hyper-rich people 'putting something back' - though this rebounded in the case of ARK, a charity run by merchant bankers and hedge fund speculators, who tried to take over Islington Green School. First on the list of ARK's sponsors is a hedge fund based in the tax haven of the Cayman Islands. Ken Muller, NUT rep at the school, confronted ARK in public: 'If you really want to help our school, *pay your taxes!*' (for more on this see Francis Beckett's book and Muller's article in the Forum special issue).

Saving the inner city

'Philanthropy' essentially involves rich men and women enhancing their self-respect and public reputation by handing back some money to the desperately poor. Whatever the motives of the individual philanthropist, it is inherently hypocritical, since philanthropists generally become rich by exploiting the poor.

Not surprisingly in our neoliberal age, Victorian philanthropy is back in fashion. Recent decades have seen a massively increased gap between rich and poor, moderated only slightly by devices such as tax credits. Around a quarter of Britain's children are growing up in poverty. The link between family circumstances/background and school achievement is extremely high, and actually increases during the years of schooling. Even those poorer children who, against all odds, are doing well at the end of primary school tend to fall behind in secondary school. A recent research report (*Wasted talent? attrition rates of high-achieving pupils between school and university*, Sutton Trust) looks at children on free meals who are among the top fifth of performers at age 11; only about a quarter of them are still among the top fifth at age 16, and only about 1 in 7 of them

Academies: privatising England's schools

reach university. New Labour is to blame both for the very slow reduction in child poverty rates and, arguably, for an education system in which poorer children are so prone to failure. Many critics ascribe some of this failure to the government's centralised control of curriculum and teaching methods, which make it difficult for teachers to connect with these young people's lives.

Against this background, the government's espousal of privatisation as the answer to 'failing schools' is problematic in several respects. Firstly, it is a diversion: the freedoms given to academies should have been given to all schools. Secondly, it continues placing blame on individual schools. Thirdly, the government are using social justice as a pretext for promoting their wider privatisation agenda.

Rather than learn from the scandals and failures of the academy project, the government are intent on accelerating it. They have identified secondary schools where fewer than 30 per cent of pupils achieve five or more A*-C grades including English and Maths. Not surprisingly, these include the majority of schools serving poorer neighbourhoods. Unless these schools can pull rabbits out of the hat very quickly, they are candidates for privatisation as academies or (an equally dubious category) 'trust schools'. Have the government considered handing back to the local authorities the academies which are failing, according to the same definition?

This so-called 'National Challenge' is a net that has been cast to catch large numbers of schools and convert them into academies; but relatively successful schools are not safe either. A notorious example is Islington Green School, serving a very deprived inner London area. The school featured on a government poster in the shape of a Tube Map, highlighting London's most successful and improved schools - but in the same week was informed that it would be closed for conversion into an academy. This was despite the fact that, against all the odds, 35 per cent of its pupils had gained five or more A*-C grades including English and Maths in 2007 - compared with the 25 per cent average for academies.

The freedom of academy sponsors to decide their own admissions policy, within the law, has enabled academies to re-engineer their school population, so that it is no longer as deprived as the school it replaced. The law forbids selection by interview, but this hasn't deterred some academies from meeting all prospective parents to warn them that their children 'won't be able to benefit' from the education offered unless they have broadband access. In other cases, expensive school uniforms and sports kit have served as a selection mechanism. In others, tests have been set on a Saturday morning a year before school transfer. Although they purport to choose a quarter of pupils from each attainment band (a so-called 'balanced intake'), the bands are reflective of divisions of the national population rather than of the local area, and this enables a school in an area where there are fewer children in the top bands to bring in more able pupils from outside. Furthermore, less informed or ambitious or well-organised families tend not to turn up for these voluntary selection tests, and are in effect de-selected. It is not surprising that, across all the academies, the proportion of pupils entitled to free meals has substantially declined.

Similarly, the freedom to exclude pupils has placed some of the most vulnerable young people at greater risk. In Middlesbrough, for example, it was discovered that the academies had expelled more pupils than all the city's other secondary schools put together.

The education of children growing up in poverty desperately needs improving, but academies are not the answer. We should be looking, for example, at the advantages of smaller and more welcoming schools, or dividing up schools into smaller communities of pupils and teachers, as in parts of Scandinavia. We need to abandon the extensive labelling and segregation of disadvantaged children as low achievers, often from the first month of primary school. We need to connect schools with communities, and enable teachers to connect with the lifeworlds of children by redesigning the curriculum and through more engaging and dialogic pedagogies.

But is it raising standards?

The government desperately needed evidence to justify their headlong rush to turn schools into academies. Their target of 200 academies was announced even before pupils who had been at the first three academies throughout Key Stage 4 had sat for their GCSEs. They therefore soon got into the situation of creating 'policy-based evidence' rather than 'evidence-based policy'. And almost immediately Andrew Adonis was announcing miraculous improvements in GCSE results. It didn't take long to dig below the surface: the academies were entering pupils for easier qualifications.

It quickly became apparent that the academies were being advised to enter as many pupils as possible for GNVQs. Indeed, almost all academy pupils were entered for at least one - a thirteen-fold increase over the predecessor schools.

Academies: privatising England's schools

The logic behind this derived from a previous government decision that a GNVQ Intermediate pass would count as equivalent to four A*-C grades at GCSE. Therefore a pupil passing GNVQ and gaining a C in any other subject would count as having jumped the magic hurdle of 'five A*-Cs *or the equivalent*'. Pupils could also repeat the GNVQ assessment tasks and tests until they passed them. (Although GNVQ has since disappeared, the scam is now re-emerging through more recent qualifications, including BTEC and literacy and numeracy tests in place of GCSE.) Neither OfSTED nor QCA have been able to provide any justification for this supposed 'equivalence'. And indeed some academy pupils were entered for three or more GNVQs as well as a range of other subjects, so clearly the notion that each was equivalent to four GCSE subjects was suspect: these pupils would have been working throughout the night. Large numbers of pupils passing GNVQ Intermediate were gaining D and E grades in most other subjects, so I tested the qualitative equivalence by making comparisons with results in similar subjects. For example, over 90 per cent of pupils with a C or higher in GCSE Science also gain A*-C in Maths, but only half of those passing GNVQ Intermediate in Science gained A*-C in Maths. Similar results emerged when comparing ICT and Maths. In general, a GNVQ pass appeared to equate to A*-E grades at GCSE, not A*-C. It should be noted that the increase in GNVQ entries did not represent an expansion of the curriculum through new subjects such as construction and engineering, but was almost entirely in Science and Computing, replacing well-established GCSEs.

Of course other schools have used the GNVQ to this effect, though to a lesser extent. By 2006, after an intensive media debate about the quality of qualifications, the government were forced to adopt a new measure: the 'five A*-Cs or equivalent' had to include English and Maths. In other words, at a minimum, a student needs a C in English and in Maths as well a GNVQ Intermediate. Three subjects is still narrow as a school leaving certificate, but it provides a rather more reliable comparison between schools.

Using this new official criterion, the academies had made a gain of 10 percentage points between 2002 and 2007 (i.e. in comparison with their predecessors' results, just before the first academies opened), from 15 per cent to 25 per cent. But since all schools nationally had improved 6 percentage points in that period, the net benefit of becoming academies over that extended period of time was only 4 percentage points (see MPs Committee of Enquiry 2007). This is a very small increase, given the money spent on construction, books and computers, and the lower proportion of poorer students in the academies (as measured by free school meals). Meanwhile, the government continued to spin to the media the story that the percentage gaining 'five A*-Cs' had doubled (using the old criterion, neglecting to explain about the GNVQ 'equivalence', and that this didn't take into account English and Maths).

This 'achievement' was at the price of a considerable curriculum narrowing, as academies were driven towards quick-fix improvements in results. Looking only at their relatively successful pupils (i.e. the 42 per cent gaining five A*-Cs or equivalent, regardless of English and Maths), Roger Titcombe and I discovered that:

only two-thirds achieved C or above in English (ditto Maths)

around half achieved this level in science

only a quarter achieved C or above in history or geography

only a quarter gained C or above in a language (indeed, only two-thirds of the academies' relatively successful pupils even studied a language at KS4)

the massive increase in GNVQ entries (more than one entry per pupil on average) was almost always in Science and ICT, i.e. existing GCSEs were being replaced with an easier qualification, rather than the curriculum being broadened to introduce new vocational choices

Breadth of curriculum was being sacrificed to quick-fix tactics to demonstrate success: these pupils would not count as well-educated school leavers elsewhere in Europe. And ironically, the academies were not providing what the Confederation of British Industry were demanding - success in core skills of literacy and numeracy, and improved vocational preparation.

The proportion jumping the new hurdle (five A*-C or equivalent including English and Maths) continues to rise, but the academies' student population is changing dramatically. Many academies have reduced the proportion of pupils on free meals; many have drawn in large numbers of pupils who would have attended other schools; and some appear to have 'lost' a significant number of pupils between KS3 tests and GCSE, whether by expulsion or by removing them from the data. Even so, some academies are desperate, and under such serious pressure to reach 30 per cent of pupils attaining 5 A*-C or equivalent, with English and Maths, that pupils have been removed from all other subjects and are cramming English and Maths all day long.

Without taking into account the factor of a less disadvantaged student population, official statistical analyses show a gain in numbers of those achieving five A*-Cs with English and Maths of only 4 percentage points beyond the improvement of other schools. This presents a problem of how to factor in the changing pupil population. National statistics show that around half of all pupils not on free meals gain five A*-Cs with English and Maths. When you factor in this figure, even the net gain of 4 percentage points disappears. But the reduction in pupils on free meals is not the only factor that needs to be taken into account when making comparisons. Perhaps more important is the influx of new pupils who are not particularly disadvantaged. In some academies, nearly half the population are newcomers, i.e. an increase beyond the number of pupils at the predecessor schools. Many of these additional pupils are the children of ambitious concerned parents who have made a positive choice in favour of the academy - hardly surprising given the hype about attainment and the impressive new buildings. Basically, after account is taken of the population change in such schools, the academies project has brought about a net improvement in attainment of *zero*. They are simply teaching different children from before.

The future

Massive pressure has been put on local councils to hand over some of their schools for privatisation. They have been threatened that their area would receive no money for new school buildings unless they handed over some schools. Only a few have been able to stand up to this blackmail. The 'consultation process' has been scandalously flawed. As the Oxford delegation to the MPs Committee of Enquiry stated:

> The academy proposals were accompanied by a vast amount of
> spin. The consultation documents were not balanced consultations
> seeking to elicit genuine views and opinions - they were more like

sales-pitches full of glitzy photographs of pupils in public schools.
More like something an expensive advertising agency would produce
(Delegation from Oxford, see Anti-Academies Alliance 2007, pp30-
31).

The local Labour MP sent a questionnaire to parents, with the following choice of
boxes to tick:

Yes, I am in favour of raising standards at Mitcham Vale and Tamworth
Manor High School by getting academy status.

No, I am against these changes to Mitcham Vale and Tamworth Manor
High Schools designed to improve examination standards.

However, resistance is growing. Local campaign groups soon formed a national Anti-
Academies Alliance (www.antiacademies.org.uk), which secured the affiliation of
the major teaching unions, Unison, UCU and others. Some local victories have been
won, though the juggernaut continues to roll.

It is impossible to predict the impact of the financial crisis on all this. Maybe
potential sponsors will realise they have more pressing concerns. Perhaps the
government will no longer be able to lavish funds on these privately-managed
publicly funded schools. Without a broad professional and public campaign,
however, it seems likely that many more schools will become academies or trust
schools.

The establishment of academies continues to be troubled, and recent news of
local victories is encouraging. A bulletin from the Anti-Academies Alliance lists the
following:

The Headteacher in ULT's Walthamstow Academy left suddenly when
NUT members prepared for a ballot. Lord Bhatia had to resign as
Chief Executive of Edutrust following financial mismanagement. The
press reported that OASIS had a 'riot' in their newly opened Mayfield
Academy, and had to sack the Head. The Head got the sack in Richard
Rose Academy in Carlisle after parent, pupil and teacher protest.

Academies: privatising England's schools

Derby, Dudley, Northampton, Sheffield and Stoke have all recently pulled back from academy plans. At their Spring Conference the Lib Dems announced they had turned against academies and now the Tories are split too.

There have been strikes by teachers in Bolton, Newham, Tamworth and Croydon. Even the government-commissioned PriceWaterhouseCoopers evaluation in November 2008 concluded: 'there is insufficient evidence to make a definitive judgement about the academies as a model for school improvement'.

The struggle against academies forms part of a wider battle. As I argued at the start of this article, privatisation isn't simply a matter of ownership and control, but about the purposes of schooling. It is self-evident that schools need to prepare young people to make a future economic contribution to society, but students are more than 'human resources'. Schools which are reduced to serving only economic goals, to the neglect of personal and cultural development and global citizenship, simply don't deserve the name of education.

Relationship and dependency in the public sphere

Tim Dartington

The importance of relationship is devalued in contemporary culture - even in health and welfare systems, where people are necessarily dependent.

———

During the last three decades dependency has become a word of contempt, as politicians and the tabloid media have demonised benefit recipients. And alongside this there has been a denigration of dependency within welfare systems, as social policy embraces opportunity and independence (though it is hard to see - just to take an example - how independent budgets can be of much assistance to people with dementia). Since the 1970s we have lived increasingly in a post-dependent society, one in which there are no longer dependable institutions that can be relied on to look after our long-term material and psychological needs. And this can be seen as part of a bigger picture, in which individual self-interest has become a sufficient explanation of socio-economic theory.

The trend away from dependency is embedded in a contemporary culture whose view of the self can be encapsulated as 'I feel therefore I am'. Far from being a triumph of the therapeutic, however, this view of the self is expressive of an individualism that denies the central value of relationships. Its shallow conception of individuality creates an opportunity for offering quick fixes (for example the claim that a short period of CBT can turn someone's life around). The obvious attractions of therapeutic self-help are mobilised to justify reforms of health and social care

Relationship and dependency in the public sphere

that are based on offering people 'opportunities' to organise their own support or recovery; while the idea that people can be whoever they want is a cover for the resort to increasingly behaviourist forms of intervention.

The social policy agenda is now focused on opportunities for self-help rather than on trying to understand the underlying structures and relationships that provide the basis for more intransigent resistances to change - such as inequality, or complex dynamics of envy or hate. Such an agenda can be concrete and positive in its promises about outcomes, and it also serves to distract from the importance of inequalities. If we can be anything we want, it does not matter so much that we or anyone else starts at a disadvantage.

This thin view of relationship can be seen in our everyday experience of being greeted by shop-workers or told to 'have a nice day': the appearance of relationship is used to achieve a business objective. 'Person-centred added value' is used to sell products or services. But to act as if we care is not a relationship, and the pervasiveness of such management techniques only further undermines our understanding of social relations.

The post-dependent therapeutic approach in mental health can be seen in the language of 'recovery'. For example: 'recovery is about people seeing themselves as capable of recovery rather than as passive recipients of professional interventions'; 'Self management may help you! Take part in the expert patients programme'. And the promise is often explicit: 'Just two and a half hours a week, for six weeks, could change your life ...'. This emphasis on self-management has many strengths - but it also involves a diminishment in the importance of relationships to others, including a reduced respect for the authority derived from the competence and experience of others. Why should I think that anyone knows better than me about anything? Isn't the customer always right?

One area where the weakness of the post-dependent approach is revealed is in discussion of what is now called the parenting deficit. The current approach to issues of parenting is constrained by the language of (children's) rights and (parental) responsibilities. This is silo thinking: look at the child over here, the parent over there. The focus is not on the relationship between them. But, as the psychoanalyst Donald Winnicott said, there is no such thing as a baby on its own, it is always in relation to its mother. Children grow within the conscious and unconscious relationships and communications of their parents and family. They cannot be separated from them. Understanding this is crucial to debates on parenting. For example, in discussing an issue such as underage drinking a psychoanalytic approach might ask about the authority of the parent in relation to the child. Instead there tends to be a - seemingly attractive - focus on mutuality: what is good for me is good for you. But this mutuality tends to be understood narrowly, in terms of exchange rather than relationship.

A culture of measuring

Public services have become caught up in this instrumental and economically driven approach, as patients and service users become customers of health and social welfare. A social policy culture that emphasises the need for measurable outcomes is a powerful managerial constraint on relationships within public service. One example of the effects of such practices can be seen in the management of care workers in relation to service users. A home care team, working in the community, is employed by the local authority; and the staff are contracted to work for a specific amount of time with each service-user, with technology allowing for each home visit to be timed to the minute. The management argues that this is a way of introducing some flexibility: the carer can give the service-user more time on a specific occasion if she needs it, and this can be monitored, with the extra time being taken from the next visit. In this way, from a management perspective, the system is being more responsive to client need and offering more flexibility - surely a good thing. But in fact this is a way of asserting more control (this is the essence of New Labour managerialism, as evidenced on a larger scale by the seemingly independent but closely regulated NHS Foundation Trusts). And somewhere along the way during this monitoring exercise the human relationship between the carer and the service-user vanishes.

The reality is that, left to themselves, some carers would do a lot more than they are contracted to do, because they get into a relationship with the service-user. Equally, other carers may exploit any lack of surveillance in the system to do less than they should. That, you might say, is human nature - the good egg/bad egg syndrome. The problem lies in the response, which has been to make them both the same: to contain the good and coerce the bad to a single standard of a National Vocational Qualification within a National Service Framework. This may be benign in its intent but it is also Orwellian in its process. In practice, it is only if it is applied in an inefficient and incomplete way that the system works with any humanity and respect for people's relationships. Some very good care is provided, but this is in despite, not because, of these safeguards. And some bad care may also remain undetected by the monitoring system.

Having tried to squeeze the life out of the relationships between carers and cared for, social policy now thinks to introduce targets for compassion. But regulation does not sit easily with the complex task of making relationships: if you allow carers to have relationships of any significance with service users, things will get messy. That which is spontaneous, idiosyncratic and uncertain in its outcome does not fit with an agenda of national standards. Thus one NHS mental health trust, taking a global view of its recruitment needs, decided to employ a significant number of staff from a country whose caring had impressed a senior manager, only to be disappointed when the caring culture did not successfully transfer into the NHS Trust. We need the remarkable competence of ordinary people to care for others; we must not be frightened of that competence and seek to impose mechanisms of control. What is needed, rather - in the supportive psychological sense - is containment.

In modern organisational life it often looks as if relationships are all important, but this is usually expressed through networks rather than through sentient one-to-one communication. And networks have the dynamics of speed-dating - they offer a quick and ready way of seeing who might suit our immediate needs. This is 'just-in-time' management applied to relationships. In public services the just-in-time-system can be seen in the increased reliance on 'bank' staff who work shifts as required - more evidence of the collapse of respect for the value of relationships.

A more relational or psychodynamic perspective is concerned with our capacity to connect with others, but the therapeutic ideal has become self-sufficiency. Some of the dysfunctional consequences of this approach can be seen in the case of one resident in an independent living scheme who was forced to carry out tasks to demonstrate her progress in being independent - by, for example, doing the washing up while two care workers stood over her. Her daughter saw this as patronising and insulting - more punishment than support - and complained to the manager. The response was that the services had to be able to show outcomes to justify their funding. On the ground, it seems that this meant standing over an old lady doing the washing up. In a care system of this kind, if a significant relationship does develop it is likely to deviate from such unthought-out protocols.

Recognition of relationships of dependency is a major casualty of the new systems. In order to play down dependency and maintain the appearance that all concerned are autonomous beings, patients and clients of public services have been re-allocated the role of service users - the therapeutic equivalent of customers, assumed to know their own needs. This has its attractions, as an attempt to ensure some parity in what is otherwise an unequal power relationship. But once patients become customers their needs can be redefined as wants. And at this point the realities of power re-enter the calculation: the providers of services are in a position to subject these 'wants' to cost benefit analysis, and to substitute alternative products. This is particularly problematic at a time when illnesses are increasingly being linked to life-style choices - obesity leading to diabetes, diet and stress being associated with cardio-vascular diseases, alcohol's association with disease, etc. Assessment processes fit uneasily in this process: assessment of need is in fact inextricably tangled with the management of resources.

The service user has to fit the criteria for the provision of the service according to a rights and responsibility framework: for such-and-such a reason the user has the right to a service, and the provider agency is commissioned to provide it. Interventions are delivered and monitored as short-term interactions. Cases are opened, shut and re-opened according to externally determined criteria. The apparent offer - the promise of a relationship - is a shallow pretence.

In this kind of regime psychoanalysis does not fare well, though in the past psychoanalytically informed thinking was part of the professional training and practice of many health service professionals. Psychoanalysis is founded in a therapeutic relationship that can last years. Its emphasis on continuity, regularity and a close attentiveness to thoughts and feelings runs counter to the modern reality of managers who are looking for 'quick wins'. From the perspective of its critics it does not seem a very efficient technique, and in a system dominated by market values of productivity it is hard to defend as best value. But at the core of this work there is a respect for the patient's own capacity for learning, and for the real human difficulties of learning and changing, which contrasts with the urgency of time-limited interventions.

Relationship and dependency in the public sphere

The need to acknowledge dependency

The intimacy of a relationship that is respectful of dependency requires an open-ended commitment, when you don't know exactly what you are getting into, or what you will get out, but you have the capacity to stick with it. We recognise dependency in the nursery and the hospice, but not in between - though there is not a time in our lives when we are not dependent on others for our survival and comfort.

The human need for relationship is not of course lost or destroyed in all these processes. As already mentioned, careworkers may demonstrate very powerfully a capacity for creating an intimate relationship outside of kin, even when the protocols do not allow it. However, the current system reinforces the capacity we all have to act all the time as if we are on our own in our achievements, and to do everything we can to defend ourselves against the sure and certain knowledge that this simply is not true, that we are truly inter-dependent. But hatred of dependency is different from denial. The hatred we can do little about, but the denial is something for us to work with in the development and management of human systems. And though we may at times deny our dependence, the entrepreneurial culture promoted by the government only suits a small minority of people - or a small part in each of most of us. The majority of us remain risk averse, having neither the stomach nor the skill to make the best of every opportunity according to a resourceful evaluative maximising model, beloved of neoliberal economic theory. Continuous effort is required to mould our interactions into instrumental forms.

The voluntary sector, with its not-for-profit organisations created and developed to give expression to deeply-held values and commitment, is also continuously suborned by an insistent demand that it becomes efficient and competitive. Chief executives move from one cause to another without noticing any conflict of interest, and having successfully competed for government funding go on to become government advisers. But below that opportunistic leadership, people continue to act on their enthusiasms as much as their interests. A partner from one of the major consultancies once explained to me how the voluntary sector did not understand the employer-employee relationship. Volunteers, local committees, ideologically driven workers, have a tendency to do what they think right, and managing them requires an empathy with the other's desires that can only be carried through by relationship. It is when that breaks down that there will be trouble and conflict.

Soundings

Modern management systems find it difficult to co-exist with an ethos that resists instrumentalisation.

The current approach to working relationships attempts to realise a relationship without dependence; it aims for a relationship of independent operators - who are nevertheless managed by surveillance and audit and a performance-related reward system. Qualities of loyalty and trust are no longer needed if their advantages can be achieved by technicalities of performance management. The quality movement introduced the concept that nothing has meaning unless it can be measured. But the concept has developed even further - so that anything that can be measured will be, even if the measurement is meaningless. This robotic tendency in human relations - to see the individual as a productive unit that can be made to run at near optimum efficiency - has led to a thriving new therapeutic culture at work, which addresses the needs of the human-in-the-robot. There are counselling services funded by employers, and - for more important people in the organisation - executive coaching. Employees who are downsized are offered out-placement services. Remuneration is increasingly linked to performance bonuses, as if the individual is a sole trader in a competitive enterprise.

The relationship of customer and provider, in so far as it exists, is instrumental - a defensive contract rather than a real engagement of identities. The power of contracts and protocols to impose behavioural norms has replaced the authority of personal relationships to develop appropriate behaviours. In the place of the uncertainty of relationship, we have got stuck in a new therapeutic culture that indulges the fantasy of personal salvation. This provides a very necessary defensive environment, psychologically speaking, where we can live without the necessity for a committed relationship: in helping us to live with the freedoms of a market economy that leave us feeling entrapped it makes the resultant world of targets and audit sort of tolerable. The freedoms of the market are, arguably, good for us as customers for cheap computers or shoes, but get us anxious, overworked or excluded in our working lives as suppliers of goods and services. Nor is it all good news for the customer. In health and social care, as we have seen, even the most vulnerable people also have to live up to the expectations of the market. In a world in which we feel increasingly impotent, the therapeutic fantasy offers the consoling prospect that we are still free men and women.

Does the end of life have to be hell?

Guy C. Brown and Sarah A. Radcliffe

Rather than solely focusing on prolonging life, we need to address the problems of chronic bodily degeneration at the end of life.

———

I s it inevitable that dying and the last few years of life are horrors? Does it have to be this way? It is tempting to think that ageing and chronic death from old age are 'natural', while acute death of the young is somehow unnatural. However, the exact opposite is the case. Significant ageing and degenerative disease are rare in wild animals, and were uncommon in humans up until two hundred years ago. Why? Because they died comparatively young, before they had time to age significantly. The average human lifespan was about thirty years before 1800, but since then has been increasing at about two years per decade in the UK. Current life expectancy is about eighty in the UK, and should reach one hundred by the end of the century. Only in the unnatural conditions of modern society and medicine can the exotic diseases and deaths of old age flourish.

Death is certainly not what it was. Life in the past was once described as 'nasty, brutish and short', but this would be a better description of death throughout most of history. The very shortness of life tended to mean that death too was short. People died either as children or in their prime, so ageing and the aged were rare. The most common causes of death were infections, violence or starvation. On the whole, death was rapid: people were fully alive one day, and fully dead the next (or at least the next month). There was relatively little grey area between life and death.

During the twentieth century the average lifespan in the world almost doubled, and people in ore affluent countries now tend to die old and slowly from degenerative diseases brought on by ageing. Until recently it was thought that humans had a maximum lifespan that we would hit at some point, as death from disease was eliminated. Many limits have been suggested, but each has been exceeded in practice. There is no sign of the rate of increase in lifespan slowing down, even in the countries of highest life expectancy. This suggests that there is no maximum human life span, or at least not one we are likely to hit soon.

That is the good news.

Unfortunately, this dramatic increase in longevity has been accompanied by no discernable change in the rate of ageing. People appear to age now at the same rate as they did two hundred years ago. But they live longer, and so they age longer, and to a greater extent, before they die. Consequently, the increase in lifespan has not been matched by an equivalent extension of healthy life: increasingly, the additional years of life we gain are associated with bodily degeneration, which translates into years spent with disability, disease and dementia. Between 1981 and 2001, life expectancy in the UK increased by four years, but healthy life increased by only two years, with the other two years being spent in ill-health. One cause of this is that the linear increase in lifespan is colliding with a roughly exponential increase in degenerative disease with age. For example, your chances of having Alzheimer's disease doubles every five years that you live beyond 65 years. One alarming result is that about 25 per cent of people in the UK currently get dementia before they die. And if current trends persist this figure is likely to rise to 50 per cent by 2050, simply because we are living longer. Thus one half of the UK population currently under the age of 40 years may get dementia before they die, unless we take dramatic action now. Are we taking action to deal with these trends? No - just the opposite: we are creating the conditions for such a social disaster.

The vast majority of people in the affluent world (and increasingly in the poorer countries of the world) die from degenerative diseases, such as cancer and heart disease. These diseases are caused by age, and dying from them is slow and is becoming slower, so that the processes of death and ageing are merging into one. Death is currently preceded by up to ten years of chronic ill health in the UK, and this figure is rising. Few people survive until death without significant physical and/or mental disabilities, extending over years. Death is no longer an event; it

Does the end of life have to be hell?

has become a long, drawn-out process. The fact that death is slower entails great challenges for ourselves, our societies and our health and care services.

Even in the absence of disease, old people progressively accumulate disabilities, including loss of sight, loss of hearing, and loss of mobility due to osteoporosis, arthritis, fractures and declining muscle strength. And even in the absence of disability, ageing brings decline in physical and mental capacities. Sight, hearing, taste and smell are dulled in everyone, and reaction times slow. Memory, IQ and linguistic ability decline; creative thinking falls off; mental productivity wanes; motivation and initiative fade away; while depression, anxiety and social isolation all increase with age.

None of this is good news, and there is no point pretending otherwise: it is one of the worst horrors of the human condition.

How did we get into this mess?

Our fear of death led us to prioritise quantity of life over the quality of life. Medicine has been oriented towards the postponement of death, no matter what the quality of life that remains. 'Life at any cost' has been the war cry, as society has attacked mortality and the acute causes of death without a parallel attack on morbidity. Huge resources are devoted to preventing infectious diseases, stroke and heart attacks in the elderly, which are arguably the least worst ways to die. Yet the consequence of these resource decisions are that people die by more protracted means, suffering years of dependency, isolation and poor quality of life. We now have the means to extend life beyond what is sensible - finding ourselves without the social, medical and political means to cope with and prevent degenerative ageing and the myriad chronic maladies associated with it. By attacking death at the end of life, we have allowed death-within-life to grow, so that the end of life is no longer worth living.

The suppressed dread of death has allowed our society to sleepwalk into a situation where people face real horrors at the end of life, simply because we cannot face dealing with the issue of how people should exit life. The ways in which we deal with degenerative ageing and those affected by extended years of illness add to the invisibility and lack of understanding of these issues. Extended, degenerative dying has generally been banished to hospitals, care homes and hospices. In hospital, doctors are bound to keep people alive at any costs, and the issue of how to care best for those with Alzheimer's, dementia and declining quality of life is inappropriately kept in a medical context, rather than being the subject of an extended social-political debate.

Medicine and medical research has had an unbalanced focus on mortality (i.e. death rates) rather than morbidity (years spent in illness). According to the 2003 World Health Report *Global Burden of Disease*, the relative contributions of different diseases to years lived with disability in the aged were: dementia (11 per cent), stroke (9 per cent), cardiovascular disease (5 per cent) and all forms of cancer (2 per cent). The proportion of research papers (since 2002) devoted to these chronic diseases reveals a starkly different ordering of priorities: cancer 23 per cent, cardiovascular disease 18 per cent, stroke 3 per cent and dementia 1 per cent. Thirty times as much money is spent on cancer research in the UK as on dementia research, yet dementia contributes five times more years lived with disease than cancer. Given these relative resource priorities, it is no surprise that cancer deaths are declining while the prevalence of dementia is climbing rapidly. It is no longer sensible to leave these resource decisions to charities and medical research boards. Society as a whole needs to have an informed debate about difficult questions, such as whether we should be reducing heart disease and cancer death rates, so that average lifespan increases towards 100 years, if that results in 80 per cent of us being cognitively impaired.

As a global society we have been remarkably successful at taming acute forms of death. Yet many acute forms of death have been converted to chronic disease or disability. Heart attacks have become heart failure; stroke has become vascular dementia; diabetes, AIDS and even some cancers have been converted from acute causes of death to chronic disabilities. All of these are great medical advances, but they have a downside: the conversion of acute (rapid) to chronic (drawn-out) death. There is a crucial economic aspect to this, as the creation of longer-living but sick patients has an up-side for the pharmaceutical companies. Of course drug companies do not set out to promote chronic disease - rather, the modern economics of drug development, through a market-led process, favours drugs that prolong disease over drugs that cure disease. Curing diseases does not pay - because you lose your patient; whereas converting an acute disease into a chronic disease pays very handsomely indeed - because you convert a short-term patient into a long-term consumer of your drugs. Development of a successful drug is thought to cost

Does the end of life have to be hell?

about $500 million. So the business plan for a miracle drug is unlikely to leave the drawing board if the patient only needs to take one pill to be cured. All the main blockbuster (i.e. economically successful) drugs, such Zantac, Viagra and anti-retroviral drugs for AIDS are blockbusters partly because the patient is not cured.

Patients, medics and funding agencies have, understandably, been more concerned to prevent early death than to prevent degenerative disease. Yet the long drawn-out death of ill and often demented people is much, much harder and more costly for the individual concerned, their family and society. So another strand of the over-due public debate about degenerative ageing has to be about care and its consequences for individuals, families and societies. Depression, anxiety and social isolation all increase with age, and this places increasing burdens on carers and relatives. Frail elderly people often want to continue to live at home in the communities where they have a social life and networks. Yet there is relatively little effective care in the community for those with degenerative ageing. And finding a care home is often difficult, hampered by the lack of places, information, and support for relatives and friends acting on behalf of the elderly person. Public discussion about the type, location and provision for this type of infrastructure is urgently required. Caring for the elderly ill has too often been an individual problem, dealt with on a case-by-case basis between family and the medical service; it needs to become a publicly acknowledged and more socialised process. Hospices provide an excellent model for palliative care of the old and dying, but because of economic constraints their services are currently restricted to those with incurable cancer who are acutely dying (i.e. they cover the last week or two of life). Hospice services need to be more widely available in the community (i.e. for those at home with a range of diseases).

The consequences for society of these social attitudes to death, and the existing medico-pharmaceutical system, are far-reaching; they impact on the ways that people must plan for their old age; how societies deal with care for the modern elderly; and the ways in which the new old are to be dealt with by politicians and government policy. This brings us to the third consequence of degenerative ageing, namely the political dimensions. How is it that the plight of the very old has been ignored for so long? In part this has to be because they are more or less invisible as voters, as a pressure group, and as a political constituency. The very old suffer from a triple burden of invisibility - the general invisibility of the old, the invisibility of the ill, and the invisibility of the non-working. In a society obsessed with the young, with the fit, and with work and play, the very old are simply invisible to public opinion, the media and political debate. The few valiant advocates for the very old who are actively involved in taking these issues to the public face an uphill struggle to make themselves heard. But - given that a substantial proportion of the UK population will get dementia before they die - the issue is not a 'minority' one. It will affect every one of us directly and indirectly. It is as significant an issue as personal pensions, and hence should engage the political will of governments, employers and ordinary individuals.

The new old

Our concept of old age is also increasingly outdated. A century ago the average lifespan in the UK was fifty years, and anyone reaching sixty years, and thus becoming 'old', had relatively few years to live. Now the average lifespan is about eighty years, so people are old for longer, old age is more heterogeneous, and the average old person is more aged. In many ways, the average person between sixty to eighty years old is much better off now than previously, because of economics, medicine and technology. But for a variety of reasons the 'new old' - those over eighty years - are in a poor way.

People aged eighty years and over now constitute nearly 5 per cent of the UK population, and are the fastest growing fraction of the population. Yet they have by far the worst health, and are probably the most poorly served by the state and society. It is tempting to think that their dire circumstances are a natural consequence of ageing, but we should recognise that in part their present problems were created by a society that extended life without making parallel efforts to reduce ageing and the diseases of ageing. It is perhaps tempting to think that the very old should be left alone, because they are going to die soon anyway, or because they are no longer contributing to society, or because there is nothing we can do about it. But we would not accept such lame excuses in relation to any other fraction of the population. We owe the very old at least as much respect and attention as the very young, if only because that is where we, and almost everyone we know, are headed.

A century ago there were around one hundred centegenarians in the UK. But now there are almost 10,000 people alive in the UK today over the age of one hundred. And the government's Actuaries Department predicts there will be astonishing 250,000 centegenarians in the UK by 2050. This sounds like a good thing. However, according to a recent MRC survey, the quality of life of these oldest old is appalling - for example 80 per cent have moderate to severe cognitive deficits. With the prospect of further ageing and degeneration among the elderly population, there is an urgent need to rethink and, arguably, reorient social, medical and political priorities.

Ten recommendations for a better end to life

Managing the compression of morbidity

The morbidity gap is the gap between average lifespan and healthy lifespan, and corresponds to the average number of years we live with chronic disease or disability. Hence the morbidity gap should be a central statistic in our society, as strategically important as GDP or inflation. Governments should commit to managing the compression of morbidity, i.e. reducing the number of years we live with disease or disability. Currently it is no-one's job to address this problem. Hospitals, health authorities, governments and the World Health Organisation do not seek to compress the morbidity gap. There is indeed considerable uncertainty and argument as to whether morbidity is increasing (expanding) or decreasing (compressing) as average lifespan increases, and the answer may well vary from country to country, and according to how we define disease and disability. Current evidence in the UK indicates that the morbidity gap is growing, but medics and governments seem happy to regard this as an inevitable consequence of an ageing population, rather than as a consequence of their past prioritisation of preventing mortality rather than morbidity. Whether morbidity is increasing or not, we must now actively seek to reduce it in the future: we must actively manage the compression of morbidity.

Funding medical research in proportion to the contribution of a disease to morbidity rather than mortality

Governments must now act to compress morbidity by increasing by several orders of magnitude the funding of research into ageing, and diseases and disabilities of ageing. That may sound economically impractical. In fact it is likely to be fiscally neutral in the short-to-medium term, and fiscally beneficial in the long term. Governments could stop their own funding of research on cancer and heart disease; this would not stop such research because it is currently mainly funded by charities. That money could then be redirected to research on ageing, and those diseases of ageing with most impact on morbidity (for example, dementia, stroke, osteoporosis). By decreasing research on the main causes of death in the aged, the increase in life expectancy could be slowed, hence reducing the expected increase in the morbidity of the aged. And by redirecting research funding onto morbidity of the aged, we could additionally reduce the massive health costs associated with that morbidity (most health care costs are spent on the last years of life). Reducing morbidity at the expense of mortality has obvious economic benefits in terms of both health and pension costs. And those economic gains could be reinvested in ageing research, until we have compressed morbidity at the end of life sufficiently to rebalance morbidity and mortality. When, in the future, the morbidity gap has been sufficiently compressed, we can begin again to reinvest in preventing mortality and extending life, because then that extended life might be worth living.

Taking ageing seriously

Research and research funding needs to be redirected to ageing and quality of life, rather than aimed simply at preventing death. We have spent two hundred years battling death, without seriously trying to change the rate of ageing. Government and private sector spending on ageing research is miniscule compared to spending on medicine. In part this may be because we believed that ageing was natural and immutable. However, as argued above, ageing is in fact unnatural, and research on other animals has shown that the rate of ageing can be slowed. It used to be thought that ageing resulted from a fixed biological programme. But most scientists now accept that ageing results from an accumulation of biochemical errors, which in principle are amenable to correction or prevention. All that is required is the political will, and a few decades of research. But we need to urgently change our priorities by putting billions of pounds, rather than millions, into ageing. The Medical Research Council (MRC), which has presided over the expansion of chronic disease in the UK, should be broken up, and a new Research Council for Ageing created, along the lines of the National Institute for Ageing, which was a success in the USA. Ageing research has had a bad press because it has been associated with the frivolous pursuit of immortality. But ageing research and gerontology are not about immortality, but rather about making life bearable at the end of life.

Creating a realistic public route to drug discovery, clinical trials and patenting

We have to develop alternative routes to drug development for therapies that don't make economic sense for the pharmaceutical and biotech industries. The NHS is the main market for drugs in the UK, and the NHS drugs bill is huge. However, the NHS, medics and the government do not determine which drugs and treatments are developed. Instead, this is determined by the market, because drug development is privatised in this country and elsewhere. The market and drugs industry, as it is currently structured, is efficient at producing certain types of treatment but not others. The NHS, universities, government research institutes and charities in the UK have an immense expertise and potential for drug development: there are alternative routes to drug development within this public sector, but they are small and under-funded. They need to be massively expanded, so that the drugs that are actually needed are developed, rather than the drugs that the pharmaceutical industry wants us to have. However, we also need to produce economic and other incentives for the private sector to seek to cure diseases and slow ageing. One of the current obstacles to drug and other medical treatment development is the patent system and intellectual property laws: this system does not allow treatments to be developed co-operatively within the public sector, or between the public and private sector. And it discourages treatments that take a long time to develop and verify, which is particularly relevant for ageing and the diseases of ageing. We need to shake up the patenting system, so that it delivers what we want, not what it can.

Replacing clinical targets for mortality rates with targets for reducing ageing/ morbidity rates

The current UK government has an obsession with health targets, but many of those targets relate to reducing causes of death, such as heart disease and cancer. The recent policy green paper from the UK Conservative party repeats the same mistake in spades, making the top health targets of the probable next government the reduction of mortality rates from cancer, heart disease and respiratory illness. However, hitting these targets is likely to decrease the health of the nation rather than increase it, unless ageing and the maladies of ageing are targeted at the same time.

Giving people the death they want

Assisted suicide, voluntary euthanasia and other forms of assisted dying should be legalised, within a tight regulatory framework. These are not general solutions to the general problem, but they are specific solutions for specific individuals in specific situations. And those difficult situations are becoming much more common as a result of society's previous choices. It is untenable for society to create the conditions for a degenerative very-old age, and then claim there is no exit strategy for the individuals concerned other than to continue degenerating. Obviously there is a quick-and-painless alternative exit strategy, and it is inhumane not to offer that alternative to those who desperately want and need it. In those countries, such as the Netherlands, that do offer this alternative, it is only used in 1-2 per cent of deaths, and it does not lead to the end of civilisation. We need also to empower advance directives (i.e. living wills), so that people get the deaths they want. Most people want to die at home, but they end up in 'homes' or hospital. We need a 'home death' or 'real death' movement, equivalent to the 'home birth' movement, to empower people at a time when they feel most powerless. Death needs to be de-medicalised as far as humanely possible, at least for those who want it that way.

Granting higher political priority and visibility to issues concerned with the quality of the end of life

This might involve giving higher status and priority to palliative care and end of life issues within medicine and care services. It is likely that more and better-funded hospices will be required, yet the public debate around how to provide these, and how they are serve their users, and be funded and managed, has still not been held. Hospices ought to be as ubiquitous and well-funded as maternity hospitals. In order to keep standards of care high and in the public eye, a system to monitor care homes could engage broad sectors of society, especially since people will realise that they might become future users. We need to think about whether the state has a higher order of responsibility for the care of those over the age of eighty years (the new old) than for those over sixty/sixty-five years, especially at a time when dementia and family fragmentation are becoming increasingly prevalent.

Creating enabling technologies for the very old

We need to think creatively about how to enable a higher quality of life for the old and very old. For instance, appropriately designed gadgets and information technologies built into the world around the old could extend their social networking, create artificial communities and permit a greater political presence. Companion technologies could also aid memory, and face recognition, and ameliorate cognitive deficits. Intelligent domestic robots could allow old people to live independently in their homes for longer. Intelligent wheelchairs integrated with power-assisted movement of limbs could facilitate the physical mobility of the aged, if they were integrated into the design of houses and communities. The design of cities, buildings (especially community-based facilities) and streetscapes should take into account the ways in which the elderly and extremely old can move around and participate in society. Designers, manufacturers and architects can also consult widely and more systematically with the elderly and their carers, in order to ensure the most appropriate technologies, materials and designs.

Making the old less invisible and enabling more realistic expectations of death and end-of-life

Many people have unrealistic expectations about death and end-of-life. So they want to stay alive at any cost to their quality of life. And in consequence, half of a lifetime's health expenditure can be spent on the last year of life, in an increasingly fruitless medicalisation of death. To change our relationship with age and death, children should be educated about end-of-life issues, through the school curriculum, student programmes and community activities. Care homes and hospices need to be brought closer to the communities they serve, through education programmes, visits, and other means. The old need to be reintegrated into society and communities in ways that are beneficial to all. In particular we should be enabling the younger old to help the older old, and more generally participate in the voluntary sector and other social roles.

Soundings

Changing our concept of death

Our concept of death, inherited from history and film, is either of violent death or of a fevered soul wracked by delirium fading into the night and expiring with a final, faint breath. This might have been the average death two hundred or four thousand years ago, but the reality now is very different. Death is no longer an event, it is a long drawn-out process. Because our concept of death is out-of-date, we still believe it is crucial to prevent death at any cost, whereas in many cases, death comes as a welcome release from the years of suffering at the end of life. That doesn't mean that assisted dying is the only solution to the problem - far from it - the solution is obviously to improve the quality of life at the end of life, by reducing the ageing, disease, disability and social isolation of modern old age.

Public service reform, the individual and the state

Hilary Cottam

Our approach to public services needs to be turned upside down, with the focus switching to relationships and networks.

———

In 2008, Participle worked with a diverse group of over three hundred older people and their families in the London boroughs of Westminster and Southwark.[1] We spent time in their homes, going shopping with them, helping with the odd job, and introducing them to one another - and gaining insight into how individuals and families see themselves, their aspirations, their dreams.

The aim of our work was to ensure a rich third age, one that every citizen might live regardless of income level or assets: a life less ordinary. In Southwark, our specific goal was the design of a new universal service that might be replicated nationally - supporting older people to live in a way of their choosing as they age. In Westminster our work has been more closely focused; we have worked only with those who define themselves as lonely, the majority of whom are over eighty and housebound, with the goal of facilitating rich social lives.

This article briefly tells the story of this work, the affordable solutions we have designed, and the nascent lessons for how we might re-think a welfare state, particularly its relationship to individuals and - most importantly of all - to wider social bonds.

Soundings

In *Soundings* 35, Zygmunt Bauman argued that a self-assertive left should measure its activities against the experience of its weakest members.[2] Those who are older, in particular the 'oldest old' and the frail, provide a good benchmark for this aspiration.

Today one in five older people are below the poverty line, and one in three report themselves as lonely. The challenge is not new. In 1948 this same figure of one in three older people reported themselves to be lonely - a matter of deep concern to William Beveridge, who felt that the failings of the post-war welfare reforms he had orchestrated were already painfully visible in such statistics.

Loneliness, however, maps uneasily onto economic deprivation, and it is not usually a central concern for public service reform. It raises questions about the role of relationships: within communities, and between individuals, the state and the market. The service-delivery mindset, which underpins so much thinking about public services, finds it hard to think about relationships between people, as opposed to targeting a 'user'. This is a deep challenge for social reform, exposing the limits of the current welfare state, and of many of the reform models on offer.

Ageing Britain

Britain is ageing. The resulting burden on pensions, health services and social care services is acute. The funding gap in social care is predicted to grow by £6 billion in the next twenty years if current eligibility criteria are maintained. Recent financial turmoil only exacerbates this gap.

In a *Guardian* article in 2007, hair-raising headlines accompanied a colour-coded map showing the levels of care available to people locally (*Guardian*, 22.11.07). Over three quarters of local councils have already reduced their help for the elderly to the point that only those with most desperate need are now eligible. As costs grow because of rising numbers, the article explained, councils will draw ever tighter guidelines around who is eligible for state support, in an effort to reduce budgets that are already spiralling out of control.

This is a narrative welcomed by the government, who believe that much work still needs to be done to 'educate' the public as to the extent of the crisis, in order that there can be a wide ranging debate and a new settlement around provision for the elderly, in a society where in the not-too-distant future three quarters of the population will be over the age of 60, and for every working person there will be two in need of support.

Seen through the lens of the state the problem looks intractable. Faced with numerical pressures there appear to be only two options. Raise taxes to pay for additional care or tighten the criteria to reduce the numbers of those eligible for care. Since it is widely believed that the general public will not tolerate increased taxes to support elder care, local government has chosen to tighten the eligibility criteria. This is in spite of the evidence that authorities that have already tightened their eligibility criteria have found it hard to make significant savings, since individuals once classified as 'moderate' usually deteriorate without support, until they are soon classified once more as needing state support.

This, then, is the widely accepted and dominant narrative on ageing in Britain. It is a story of a demographic time bomb, a story of the state failing numerous individuals. If we invert the telescope, however, and look from the perspective of individuals themselves, a very different story emerges.

In Britain, people over sixty hold 80 per cent of the nation's wealth - valued at £1.3 trillion worth of assets at the start of 2008. Although the financial crisis has subsequently diminished this total, the share of national wealth remains the same amongst this population group - however unevenly distributed. Perhaps even more importantly, this expanding proportion of the nation's population make enormous social contributions (an estimated £24 billion in unpaid work), and are a rich pool of talent, human resource and often - that most scarce of commodities - time.

One thing is clear: older people have assets which dwarf those of the state. Supporting an ageing society thus needs to start with older people, and to think differently about their relationship to the state, each other and the wider community of which they are an all too often invisible part. This has been the premise of Participle's recent work, and our starting point has been to work with older people themselves.

Personal perspectives

Through working closely with older people we have observed a number of deeper issues of dependency and inequality that are not tackled by current provision - even before cuts are made.

On the walls of our small studio in South London we have portraits of some of the participants in our project, revealing the rich variety of their lives and experience. Shirley, 60, is seen dating internationally on Skype. Robert, 65, is photographed dancing with his small daughter: he became a first-time father in the same month he started to draw his pension. People are living longer and many are inventing new ways of doing it: taking advantage of technology, better health, rich social lives and the opportunity to travel.

Also on our walls is a picture of Steve, 55, who spends most of his days in the pub. He is bored and very overweight, and last month was diagnosed with diabetes and a series of other health problems. Steve's story, as he himself recognises, is different: it is a story of impending crisis, a story that personally mirrors that which is told nationally through statistics. For individuals such as Steve, the concept of a third age - that supposed golden period between retirement and a frail older age - is mythical. His path will be one of a shift from a lifetime on low-paid work, followed by incapacity benefit, into an immediate, long and painful decline. This will be costly for the state and painful for Steve.

Conversations also reveal disappointment with the quality of services offered. There is resentment at technocratic delivery: what is sought are relationships. From the perspective of the householder, the voluntary sector - whilst sometimes praised for individual services - is tarred with the same brush; too often it refers an individual to yet another service, rather than offering any real help, and it frequently shares very closely in the technocratic culture. As the voluntary sector has been increasingly locked into bidding for contracts from the local authority, the personal touch and creative élan that once characterised many organisations has tended to be lost.

In the same authorities there is a parallel story of wealth and assets - in time and talents as well as in finance and equity (largely wrapped up in housing). One of the things we have been told most loudly is how much people want to give and contribute. But most are locked out, occasionally consulted as 'users', but never conversed with as individuals and communities.

Most people's needs are small and episodic: someone to go up a ladder once in a while, advise on how to use a new bit of technology, go through financial statements once a quarter, or offer support with a new situation. If left undone, apparently small things build up, until the state needs to come in with a blanket and expensive response. Once state help is provided, people tend to hang on to it. A hoarding mentality is common: resources are known to be scarce, and hard to come by in the first place, so people hang on to things they don't need, just in case.

Those with the strongest social connections to friends, family and neighbours are able to meet most if not all of their smaller needs before they become insurmountable. The increasing importance of social connections was clear from the earliest stages of our work, as were the challenges that many face in maintaining or making these connections. Many years of caring for a partner leave great numbers isolated and needing to start again at the very moment (the death of a loved one) when they feel most frail and vulnerable. Older people we worked with, whether because of their age or the generation to which they belong, often valued a smaller number of deeper relationships, which left them more vulnerable to isolation as others died or moved away.

As resources have become ever more restricted, however, the state has emphasised the provision of personal care services over any activity that might form greater social connections, making individuals ever more dependent on the state. This is most clearly seen in the provision of day-care centres, to which individuals very often have to be bussed, at high cost. Whilst time spent in these largely desolate places might be important relief for carers, those who visit them are unlikely to make any bonds with people who might be able to help them outside the centre, or to strike up more regular friendships, given the distance that day-centres are from people's homes.

It is as if the state is investing in making itself not only the provider of solutions but the friend to the elderly. It is a story of relationships in the wrong place

Making patterns

Very early on we saw patterns amongst those we met. The state relies on four categories to segment need (based almost entirely on finance and physical ability), and spends up to 80 per cent of the resources available on sorting individuals into these categories. We saw that old people themselves see their lives in terms of interests, skills, openness to new things and relationships past or present. Patterns in terms of attitude and outlook - which most determined the quality of life an older person was living - were largely independent of wealth or income, and did not correlate with 'needs' as traditionally understood by the state. Most simply, we were able to think of the people we had come to know along two continuums. One of these plotted their agency - their willingness to try new things; the other plotted their interests. It was clear that we would need different starting points or conversations depending on where an individual might be along a continuum.

We also understood what would be the components of any new universal service: practical help, social connections and a purpose for the second half of life. We began to put together the elements of a new universal service and to try them out in practice: the elements that would become Southwark Circle. In Westminster we began to try out a new service to connect the lonely and the housebound, a service we have called Meet Up.

Southwark Circle

Southwark Circle is a membership organisation: a nominal monthly fee makes it open to all. Combining elements of a co-operative, a concierge service, a self-help group and a social club, the Circle changes the locus of decision-making, starting with its individual members and journeying with them, as their needs change. An expanded resource base is created through drawing on the skills of members, the voluntary contributions of neighbours, private money (from wealthier older people and their families) and state resources better deployed. Southwark Circle is a platform for new and existing services: a place that can draw together the best the state and the voluntary sector have to offer, combining them with new offers such as a film club, gardening and household services.

Meet Up

The Meet Up Service creates and supports resilient social networks. There are four elements to the service: introductions (taking into account location and the importance of the first hundred yards); phone groups (topics include music, films and current affairs); trips and transport (based on scooters and a taxi card scheme); and activities at home. The service has been designed specifically to overcome the barriers of decreased physical mobility, and early take-up of the service has been concentrated on the housebound and mobility impaired, although there is nothing to prevent those who are younger joining in. For Westminster Council this preventative service has proved attractive through its ability to reduce costs in other areas.

Beveridge 4.0

If the issues around an ageing society illustrate the biggest problems of the welfare state - the underlying inequalities, costs and dependencies, and the fissures that have developed between people - they also show the route to the fashioning of a very different model. We call the set of principles on which our new model depends Beveridge 4.0, in recognition of the fact that any new settlement must be as ambitious and bold as the original welfare settlement, but, equally importantly, that 'room, opportunity and encouragement' must be kept for voluntary action and the power of the citizen (as Beveridge acknowledged in his third and last report, towards the end of his life).

There are five key shifts which underpin Southwark Circle (and to a smaller extent Meet Up) - and potentially a future welfare state. They are as follows: a focus on building capabilities (as opposed to meeting needs); an emphasis on universal services; a definition of resources which goes beyond the current limited financial models; national platforms that support highly distributed, local responses; and an emphasis on social networks that understand the individual and their needs within a web of relationships.

Capabilities

Beveridge 1942 was a needs-based model. The focus was on the five giants of want, disease, ignorance, squalor and idleness. Clearly many of these giants, although differently labelled today, remain as significant as ever. More important than the definition of the giants, however, is the underlying philosophy of need. Our work inverts this model and focuses on assets. Specifically, the cultivation of three capabilities: learning and work; relationships; and the environment. (The capabilities approach, drawn from the work of Amartya Sen and Martha Nussbaum, has been used to underpin the Swedish welfare state.)

Older people have much to offer the labour market, and are often interested in teaching and learning. At the level of the household, this was what people wanted to discuss - the jobs they wanted to do, whether paid or voluntary, the courses they wanted to take, the skills they thought they could pass on to others. Southwark Circle will go some way to addressing this demand: members will volunteer and be paid for their work. The focus will be on supporting those who so desire to enter the labour market, against the grain of age prejudice. Making connections to platforms such as the School for Everything and Pune University will open up learning opportunities.

Ideally one imagines that relationships are something there might be time for in the third age. The story is more complex however. Geographical mobility means that many older people are living at considerable distance from their families. Our work built a strong picture of concerned adult children who would like to ensure different lives and provision for their parents as they become more frail, but are unsure where to turn. Stable communities of face-to-face relationships are also harder to find. Any response within the new social state needs to provide the tools for social participation - between older people, across generations and across spatial divides.

Southwark Circle places the need for relationships at the heart of its offer. This starts with those who work for the Circle, and a business model that prioritises face-to-face interactions and personal stability - seeing the same person again and again; and there is also a cost model that does not penalise a frontline worker for having a cup of tea and a chat. A relationship mindset also pervades every aspect of the offer - helping connect older people to their relatives in new ways; helping navigate feelings of insecurity around young people; developing involvement in neighbourhood schemes; or understanding what will keep a volunteer. Borrowing and adapting from different places - within Britain and globally - has been critical to the development of the service. The neighbourhood scheme draws on neighbourhood watch, and the inter-action skills offer draws on a Norwegian service offered to old people.

Environmental concerns of old people tend to focus on place and neighbourhood. A recurring theme in our work has been the need to make older people publicly visible, and the tangible ways in which broader issues of social participation and wellbeing are linked to the physical environment - for example the quality of the pavements, the availability of benches and toilets. Fear, particularly of the younger generation, is also a strong determinant of lives. Southwark Circle will call people when they return home, for example, because we have learnt that the fear of returning to an empty house will stop an older person doing something they would otherwise very much like to do.

Universal services

A rich third age depends on being physically active, socially engaged and maintaining a range of interests. Thus the more heavily and widely members use Southwark Circle, the richer the lives of Southwark residents will be - and, from the perspective of the Council, fewer expensive curative-type services will need to be called on

If services are protective and preventative it follows that they must be open to all and aspirational - in the sense that everyone can and wants to join. Ageing is a good example of the need for such services, but similar motivational issues underpin effective preventative health work, future climate change solutions and many aspects of Participle's work with youth. The design of universal services in turn leads to a very different way of thinking about resources, and the economics of service provision.

A new contributory principle

Ageing is currently framed as a narrative about fiscal deficits, when it needs to be about social contribution. The current narrow financial focus, which links an individual's entitlement to benefits to a system that focuses on National Insurance contributions, extends into and limits the consideration of the nature of services required and how they might be paid for. In this context, individual budgets, whose 'uncertain' merits were discussed by Peter Beresford in *Soundings* 40, can be seen as still rooted in the old economy. They might bring benefit to some, but most will find they are not eligible, since budgets will be linked to a residual model.

Southwark Circle expands the definition of, and access to, the resources available. Our work in this area contributes to a number of similar innovations taking place internationally, from participative budgeting in Porto Alegre in Brazil to experiments with voluntary financial contributions in Bogota in Colombia. When considered together this work poses a bigger challenge to the framing of public service debates.

Soundings

Distributed institutional networks

Our existing welfare state and public services operate on highly centralised principles. The current debate about devolving more power to local institutions, whilst welcomed, does not get to the heart of the matter, since it still perceives a world in which things are largely done *to* and *for* people and communities. The only difference is that now local, rather than national, government will be 'doing' it.

More bottom-up, participative approaches depend on, and are sustained by, a more distributed model. Ivan Illich described how 'good institutions encourage self-assembly, re-use and repair': 'They do not just serve people but create capabilities in them, and support initiative, rather than supplanting it'. Southwark Circle is at once hyper-local and national/international (combining street-level support with specialised or collective macro support), and works on just such a philosophy. The more it is used, the more sustainable it becomes, as expertise and resources are distributed amongst the members.

Such distributed solutions radically change the nature of the relationship between the individual and the state. At the local level, interaction is more 'human' and personal; collaboration is more feasible; and a genuine conversation around issues of priorities and contributions becomes possible, further reinforcing relationships. Finally, it is important to note that these distributed institutions will be infrastructure-light, in contrast to their 1950s predecessors - critical in a time of financial scarcity.

Social networks

Our lives are greatly determined by social networks: those of us who have strong bonds with families and friends tend to live longer and happier lives. One of the most striking insights from our deep participative work with older people, their families and social networks has been the discovery of the extreme difficulty experienced by many adult children in ensuring that their ageing parents and neighbours have the provision they need. Most adult children live at a distance from their ageing parents, which makes caring for them even harder. Strikingly, even so-called 'self-funders' - those that do not need help from the state but are looking to buy help in the private care market - face the same issues.

Public service reform, the individual and the state

People want to support each other but the systems and services on offer make this hard, if not impossible. Southwark Circle inverts the traditional hierarchy of needs. The current hierarchy helps people with their basic material needs, but sees their social life and social connections as 'nice to have', but not as an essential part of the picture. We have seen that using limited resources to enable a social life has the effect of expanding the resources available: the time and talent of friends, neighbours and family can more than meet the material needs. In other words, connecting people starts to re-configure the possibilities.

Conclusion

Participle's work starts with people and their communities, putting the individual rather than the state at the centre. Seen from this angle, it is the state that is lonely - at arms length from the communities it could serve, unable to tap the energy, skills and resources of individuals and often threatened by individuals' attempts to make meaningful social bonds with each other.

The current crisis is a moment of opportunity. We have been faced by two dominant, atomising narratives: the market telling us that we are individual consumers defined by our desires and wants, the state telling us that we are individuals defined by our needs. If there is one message that we have heard most loudly in our work it is this: even in the most 'difficult' of places and of life's stages, we want to be socially connected and to collectively contribute and make change happen. Above all we want not to be lonely and in this desire lies a set of principles to guide a very different model of public service reform.

———

Notes

1. For more information on Participle see www.participle.net.

2. Available online at www.lwbooks.co.uk/journals/articles/bauman07.html.

UK food security

Robin Maynard

Peak oil, climate change and unstable commodity prices mean that British agriculture is in need of a radical transformation.

———

Until recently, anyone raising concerns about the UK's food security with government ministers and policy-makers was likely to be dismissed as an anti 'free-trade' xenophobic crank, harking back to the days of the last war, when German U-boats threatened to cut-off our supplies of food and fuel - the majority of which were still being convoyed in from our former colonies.

The U-boat torpedoes focused public and political attention on the need for maintaining a significant strategic resource of home-grown production, and after the war, public subsidies and research and development funding were poured into agriculture. Farmers were encouraged to modernise, mechanise and become specialised arable or livestock producers, and to shift away from what was seen as inefficient, sentimentalist 'Old McDonald-style' farming - where each farm ran a mix of different enterprises. In tandem with this increased specialisation went a much greater reliance on off-farm inputs of chemical fertilisers, pesticides and pharmaceuticals for livestock. Yields and overall productivity were boosted: the proportion of foodstuffs consumed in Britain that are home-grown has risen from the pre-war total of around 30 per cent to over 70 per cent today. And alongside this production-focused push, the agri-businesses - which supplied the agrochemicals and other inputs that farmers could afford because of public subsidy - also boomed.

Superficially this policy-driven farming renaissance was a triumph of technological achievement, with greater quantities of food being produced at affordable prices for the British public. And for the past sixty-years, ensuring

UK food security

plentiful 'cheap food' has been the goal of successive governments, whatever their political leanings. But this single-minded focus on squeezing out maximum tonnes of grain or head of livestock per hectare has not been without controversy or cost - for wildlife, animal welfare and the livelihoods of rural people. The damage to wildlife habitat and diversity has been well rehearsed: 95 per cent of Britain's wildflower-rich meadows have been ploughed-up and sprayed out since 1945. And initiatives or regulation to counter the damage have been limited in their ambition and effects - as, for example, the modest schemes whereby farmers are rewarded for looking after wildlife rather than destroying it, brought in after years of campaigning by conservation groups. Even major human health scares such as mad cow disease - linked to the intensive farming practice of feeding ground-up cattle and sheep remains back to vegetarian livestock as protein - have only resulted in minor adjustments to the dominant industrial food production model. For the majority of food production across most of the world, 'business as usual' has continued. However, over the past couple of years several factors have come together to call into question the long-term sustainability of this system, forcing the issue of food security higher up the agenda - in affluent countries such as the UK as well as in the countries in Africa, Asia and Latin America that are familiar 'poster-boys' of famine and poverty.

From 2006 to 2008 global food prices rose rapidly, fuelling social and political unrest in 14 countries worldwide - causing 'tortilla riots' in Mexico and protests over the price of pasta in Italy. In the UK food price inflation has been a problem since June 2008, and growing public and media interest has at last provoked some welcome activity from government. Indeed, the first review Gordon Brown commissioned on becoming prime minister was a Cabinet Office Strategy Unit analysis of food issues generally. Their initial report, circulated in January 2008, concluded that 'existing patterns of food production are not fit for a low-carbon, more resource-constrained future'; and that 'existing patterns of food consumption will result in our society being loaded with a heavy burden of obesity and diet-related ill health'.

Strangely, those strong statements were air-brushed out of the final report published later that same year and the Strategy Unit's analysis appears to have become a 'minority report'. It seems that the hand of the Treasury and its 'free-market' inclinations have been the major steer over policy. The government's dominant view remains that expressed by Defra Minister Margaret Beckett in March 2006:

> We do not take the view that food security is synonymous with self-sufficiency ... It is freer trade in agriculture which is key to ensuring security of supply in an integrating world. It allows producers to respond to global supply and demand signals, and enables countries to source food from the global market in the event of climatic disaster or animal disease in a particular part of the world ... it is trade liberalisation which will bring the prosperity and economic interdependency that underpins genuine long term global security.

Such faith in the capacity of the 'global market' and 'trade liberalisation' to meet our food needs pervades Defra's later 2008 report, *Ensuring the UK's Food Security in a Changing World*, as evidenced in its statement that 'because the UK is a developed economy, we are able to access the food we need on the global market'.

Global food markets under stress

But the world has changed dramatically since that statement was written, and over-reliance on the global food commodity market is now as imprudent as reliance on global financial markets. Indeed, global food and finance markets are prey to the same self-serving interests; and some of the rise in global food prices stems from speculators moving out of dodgy 'derivatives' into more substantial, less toxic, food commodities. But there's a wider range of more enduring factors that are destabilising the world food market. These include the diversion by the US - once the world's major exporter of grains - of nearly 20 per cent of its cereal harvest into biofuel. The amount of grain needed to fill the tank of a typical American SUV would meet the annual needs of one hungry person in many of the poorer countries of the world.

Such factors may seem distant and irrelevant to UK shoppers and politicians, who see no apparent shortages on supermarket shelves. But there are indications that our food system's links into the global food market are showing signs of stress. Take this comment from a leading UK retailer in response to a recent food-chain

UK food security

stakeholder survey on UK food security:

> A sense across the global supply chain that, whereas in the past, as a
> retailer, we have been able to shift very rapidly between countries if
> there was a problem ... there is now a recognition that the ability to
> hop between countries is being constrained, as climate change and
> other issues, such as the price of oil, kick in ... a growing awareness
> in the food industry that things aren't going to be the same in the
> future.

That uneasiness hasn't yet filtered through to government. Simply based on the
statistics, UK food security seems robust, with the country in a stronger position
than sixty years ago, when only 30 to 40 per cent of all food eaten here was
grown in UK soils. According to Defra's statistics, the UK is currently 74 per cent
self-sufficient in indigenous foodstuffs (the sort that can be grown here), and 60
per cent self-sufficient for all foods (in other words, 40 per cent of our food is
imported). Those figures may seem reassuring - if they are accurate. In a separate
discussion paper on the origins of food consumed in the UK, the 'official self-
sufficiency figure' given for the UK was 49 per cent; and these figures were based
on the monetary value of imported and home-grown food rather than on volume
or calorific (food energy) levels. This means that the figures do not represent 'real'
edible self-sufficiency - or give a true picture of whether or not the UK is well-
placed to feed its citizens securely and nutritionally. Another Defra study states that,
overall, UK self-sufficiency has fallen by 10 to 15 per cent over the past twenty
years.

Government statistics reveal not just a widening trade gap, but also a disparity
between policies. Healthy eating guidelines urge consumers to eat more fruit and
vegetables, yet 90 per cent of fruit eaten in the UK is produced overseas, and the
area of UK land put down to vegetables has declined by nearly 25 per cent over the
past ten years. And this cannot be attributed to growing consumer tastes for exotic,
non-native fruits, or explained away as less land being needed because of more
efficient methods to grow the same amount of vegetables. Production volumes have
fallen for many indigenous British fruits and vegetables. In 2005, the UK had the
largest trade deficit of any EU country in trade with countries outside the EU (£5.35
million). But Defra's response to any food security concerns raised by this trade

gap is to argue that the majority (68 per cent) of UK imports comes from other EU member states, and it considers these countries as 'low-risk, stable trading partners'.

Defra dismisses any suggestions that a greater proportion of UK home-grown food might be a good idea by describing self-sufficiency as 'an illusion' - because it doesn't take into account the extent to which goods produced in the UK depend on imported inputs, notably oil and gas, fertiliser, pesticides, feed and machinery. In a 2005 paper, the government estimated that in the UK 69 per cent of pesticides and 63 per cent of primary energy used for agriculture were imported; and a 2006 paper put the import figure for fertiliser at 37 per cent, up from around 10 per cent in the 1970s. This is a self-defeating argument, however, as those alleged 'low-risk' EU countries who export food to us are producing food via unsustainable systems just like our own - predominantly dependent on imported, oil-based and finite mineral inputs.

And that fact - given the 'new fundamentals' of climate change and its cousin 'peak oil' - unravels any claim that the UK and the EU are removed from global food security concerns. Farming and food production in the UK, as well as globally, are simultaneously contributors to climate change and vulnerable to its impacts. Ironically, the richer countries that have pursued the path of industrial agriculture and its associated more centralised food distribution and retail systems may well be more vulnerable in the long term than the countries in the South that are popularly associated with food insecurity, poverty and famine.

Fossil fuels and finite resources

'Westernised' agriculture's increased productivity over the past sixty years has been due to a greater reliance on artificial inputs (particularly nitrogen fertilisers) and machinery, rather than on fertility-building crop rotations and livestock manure (and this has also conveniently displaced human labour). Use of fertiliser on its own is believed to have boosted crop yields by 30 to 50 per cent. But though there have long been concerns over the role of fertiliser in polluting water sources, the overall sustainability of its use has only recently been called into question. Now, in recognition that it is the main source of greenhouse gases emitted by agriculture, it is coming under much greater scrutiny:

UK food security

> With all the attention paid to carbon dioxide in the climate change
> debate, we are neglecting an impending crisis caused by the
> accumulation of man-made nitrogen compounds in the environment
> … The main nitrogen sources are agricultural fertilisers and pollutants
> in fossil fuels. The public does not yet know much about nitrogen,
> but in many ways it is as big an issue as carbon, and due to the
> interactions of nitrogen and carbon, makes the challenge of providing
> food and energy to the world's peoples without harming the global
> environment a tremendous challenge (James Galloway, environmental
> sciences professor, quoted in the *Financial Times*, 16 May 2008).

Unlike other sectors of the UK economy, in agriculture only 13 per cent of
greenhouse gas emissions are in the form of carbon dioxide. Instead, the majority
of emissions are made up of nitrous oxide and methane - with nitrous oxide
representing the larger part of this, at around 50 per cent, while methane emissions
make up 36 per cent. The main source of nitrous oxide is artificial nitrogen
fertiliser, upon which non-organic farming in the UK is dependent - it uses over 1
million tonnes annually. Nitrous oxide is 310 times more damaging than carbon
dioxide. The manufacture of nitrogen fertiliser also accounts for the biggest portion
of energy used in agriculture, amounting to over 40 per cent of all UK farming's
energy requirement. To make a single tonne of nitrogen fertiliser takes a tonne
of oil and 108 tonnes of water - in the process giving off over 7 tonnes of carbon
dioxide-equivalent greenhouse gases. But emissions from the manufacture and
delivery of nitrogen fertilisers are not included in the total for farming's official
carbon footprint: instead they are allocated to 'industrial sources'. Yet modern
industrial farming couldn't function without them. Adding them to the total boosts
agriculture's total greenhouse gas emissions by 14 per cent.

In October 2008, Ed Miliband, the new Energy and Climate Minister, accepted
the recommendation of the Committee on Climate Change to set the higher target
of 80 per cent cuts in greenhouse gas emissions by 2050 - and that this target
should include all greenhouse gases, not just carbon dioxide. That policy decision
alone questions the resilience of our current food and farming system: it would
necessitate a radical change in how we grow, source and distribute our food.
Getting anywhere near achieving 80 per cent cuts on agriculture's greenhouse gas
emissions must mean radically cutting artificial fertiliser use, as well as generally

reducing dependency on oil.

This is not simply an issue of climate change, however: in the long-term, global resources of oil are going to become scarcer, and more costly to extract. With oil prices dropping back from their high of $140 a barrel in summer 2008, the shock of peak oil may seem to have receded into the distant future. But the respected think-tank Chatham House predicts that prices will rise again over the next two decades, to £200 a barrel. Our food is steeped in oil. It requires 400 gallons of diesel to produce, process and distribute the average American's annual food intake - and a similar figure applies here. As the era of 'cheap oil' comes to an end, so too will the era of 'cheap food'.

The illusion of endlessly available fossil-fuel inputs has for a long time masked the fundamental link between good soil husbandry and sustained food security. The UN Environment Programme estimates that nearly 2 billion hectares of land are affected by human-induced soil degradation; and it gives the shocking statistic that half of the world's current arable land will be 'unusable' by 2050. And these barren acres are not confined to the global south. The European Agricultural Conservation Foundation estimates that soil erosion and degradation affect approximately 157 million hectares of land in Europe (16 per cent) - roughly three times the total land area of France.

The problem of land shortages is giving rise to a new form of colonialism, whereby richer countries that are already at the margins of viable food production, because of climate and water availability, are buying or leasing land in poorer countries. Countries purchasing 'ghost-acres' overseas to feed their populations include Saudi Arabia, Kuwait and Qatar, which are awash with oil revenues but poor in fertile land, and China, which has a burgeoning population to feed and has surpluses from its export earnings from cheaply-produced manufactured goods. Cruelly, some of the countries entering such agreements are some of the poorest in the world, such as Sudan or Madagascar, a substantial proportion of whose indigenous people are dependent on international food aid.

Meanwhile, in the UK we have lost hundreds of thousands of people from the land - and with them the skills to work it - displaced by chemicals and machinery. UK agriculture has seen a long and steady decline in employment. In 1900 around 40 per cent of the population was still employed in agriculture; by the start of the second world war that had fallen to some 15 per cent; today it's less than 2 per cent. Yet any form of lower-carbon farming - less reliant on climate-change boosting fertilisers and fossil-fuels - will certainly need more people to become involved once again in food production. Exactly how many isn't known, but the experience of Cuba offers a salutary 'real world' case-study. When the Soviet Union collapsed in 1991, Cuba's imports of agrochemicals and oil ended almost overnight. The country therefore had no option but to pursue lower-carbon, organic, more labour-intensive food production. It has since then succeeded in achieving a reasonable level of food security, but this has required the diversion of some 15 to 24 per cent of its population to the growing of food.

The loss of people with the skills or inclination to work in agriculture has been accompanied by a parallel reduction in rural infrastructure: local food shops, greengrocers, butchers and bakers have disappeared - with 1000 such shops closing every year during the 1990s. This dismantling of regional food infrastructure has contributed to the 23 per cent greater distance our food now travels in comparison with three decades ago. And the concentration of slaughter and processing plants into fewer, bigger, sites, which means that livestock travel the length and breadth of the country to slaughter, increases the risk of contamination and the spread of disease, as was the case with the 2001 Foot and Mouth outbreak. Furthermore, as our food moves further and faster between suppliers and retail outlets, lower quantities are held in store: 'low-inventory' logistics systems maximise profitability for supermarkets. But they also reduce regional food resilience and increase our vulnerability to unexpected disruptions - as happened in the Fuel Protest of 2000, when lorry-drivers blockaded food and fuel depots in protest at rising fuel costs. This minor shock to the system revealed our food system's dependency on oil and long-distance transport, and the lack of local, accessible food production in our towns and cities. As food distribution ground to a halt, panic-buying set in, and those seemingly abundant shelves quickly emptied. London was within three days of running out of food. The government's emergency Cobra Committee was convened, and the capital came close to testing out MI5's maxim that society is only ever 'nine meals away from anarchy'.

The need for major social, cultural and dietary change

The opportunity and foundations for building a different system of farming, food production and distribution, capable of delivering more resilient, sustainable food security - both in the UK and in the rest of the world - do exist. Through avoiding mainstream agriculture's addiction to artificial fertilisers, many people are actively cutting their carbon-footprint and reducing their reliance on oil. Organic farming is one of the better-known, practically available and commercially viable ways of doing this: despite the worst efforts of vested interests in agribusiness to dismiss its capabilities, organic farming received a strong endorsement in the recent International Agricultural Assessment of Science, Technology and Development. This assessment, produced by more than four hundred scientists, and signed up to by more than sixty governments (including that of the UK), concluded that:

> ... despite significant scientific and technological achievements in our ability to increase agricultural productivity, we have been less attentive to some of the unintended social and environmenta. consequences of our achievements.

> Business as usual is no longer an option ... Policies that promote sustainable agricultural practices ... stimulate more technology innovation, such as agroecological approaches and organic farming to alleviate poverty and improve food security.

This view was reinforced by a recent survey by the UN Environment Programme in East Africa of 114 projects in 24 African countries, which found that yields had more than doubled where organic, or near-organic practices, had been used; and that this increase in yield jumped to 128 per cent in east Africa. The survey also found that more than 90 per cent of the organic or near organic agriculture case studies brought benefits for soil fertility, water control, water table levels, carbon sequestration and biodiversity, thereby allowing farmers to extend the growing season in marginal areas. Head of the UN's Environment Programme Achim Steiner, and Secretary-General of UNCTAD Supachai Panitchpakdi, state in the report's executive summary: 'The evidence presented in this study supports the argument that organic agriculture can be more conducive to food security in Africa than most conventional production systems, and that it is more likely to be sustainable in the long-term'. Contrary to the strident attacks of the agribusiness lobby, who hope to offload chemicals and patented GM seeds onto less powerful countries under the gloss of 'feeding the world', agroecological systems such as organic farming can deliver a more sustainable alternative, by building farmers' independence through skills and knowledge rather than dependence on products.

In 2008 the Soil Association commissioned the Centre for Agricultural Strategy at Reading University to answer the question 'how much food could be produced in this country if all domestic agriculture were organic?' Using actual farm business data, the analysis reflected a straightforward projection of the likely immediate effect on current production volumes of the major agricultural commodities if all non-organic agriculture switched to organic. The broad answer was that, while a wholesale conversion to organic would not produce the same volume of the same food commodities as currently, for certain sectors volumes of production would increase - for example, beef, sheep, mixed cereals and oats; for some it would produce the same amount - for example fodder beans, peas and potatoes; and in others there would be big declines - for example in intensive pork and poultry meat production, which organic standards would not permit - and which (unlike grass-fed beef and sheep) is dependent on imported animal feed. The researchers also noted that any 'significant movement' in the dietary habits of the UK public towards World Health Organisation healthy-eating guidelines - which would lead to marked reductions in the consumption of meat, sugar, fats, eggs and dairy products, and an increase in the consumption of horticultural crops, root crops and minor cereals - would favour organic farming.

However, this rapid and inevitably incomplete gallop through global food security issues must not leave readers with the impression that the necessary transition to lower-carbon, more localised food and farming systems will be easy. The social, cultural and dietary changes required are enormous. Take London alone. In 2003 an analysis of London's overall 'footprint' by the Greater London Authority estimated that to supply all of Londoners' current needs the city's total 'footprint' was 48,868,000 global hectares (gha), or 6.63 gha per capita. And London's food requirements alone accounted for 41 per cent of that - at approximately 20,035,000 hectares, 2 million more hectares than the UK's total available farmland. The capital's true global 'fairshare'- i.e. its share if it reflected London's portion of the world's 'biocapacity' - would be a total footprint of 1,210,000 gha or 0.16 gha per capita. To achieve this would require all Londoners to consume 70 per cent less meat, eat more than 40 per cent local, seasonal unprocessed food, and cut their food waste by one tonne a year. This is indicative of the scale of the challenge in any wholesale switch to a more resilient, climate-friendly system.

The Centre for Agricultural Strategy's research was based on farming the same area of productive farmland as currently. But if sea levels rise, this area will decrease significantly. The pre-Copenhagen summit gathering of climate scientists in March 2009 revised the International Panel on Climate Change's previous estimates of sea-level rise by the end of this century to over a metre (the previous estimate was between 26 and 86 cm). With 57 per cent of Britain's best Grade 1 farmland lying below sea level, this revised estimate of sea-level rise brings significantly increased risks of flooding and saline incursion onto farmland, especially in East Anglia and most notably the Fens, which hold 37 per cent of England's acreage for outdoor-grown vegetables. One analysis suggests that, because of flooding, arable farming might become unviable on 86 per cent of the Fens, 10 per cent of the remainder of East Anglia, and 7 per cent of the North West. With the cost of a mile of sea-defences estimated at £6 million, it's questionable whether the UK can afford to create a gigantic walled garden in the east of the country.

Given these challenges, perhaps there is some justification for Defra's strategy in basing our food security on a significant portion of imports - though the volume, nature and source of these requires much more discussion. The Soil Association is not proposing that the UK should become 100 per cent self-sufficient in all the food we consume. If this strategy was pursued, our diet would be duller and lacking in some key additional nutrients, even if we took advantage of the much wider range of fruit and vegetables that can be grown here but are rarely seen in the shops. Tea, coffee, chocolate and bananas have become 'staples' in many people's shopping baskets, and when fairly-traded these products provide vital income and livelihoods to farmers in less affluent countries. And other imported foods, which can't be grown in the UK, form a central part in the diets of the wide range of ethnic groups that now make up British society. Furthermore, from a food security perspective importing a certain proportion of our food is a sensible hedge against disease outbreaks or crop failures arising from unanticipated weather events. But, equally, it makes strategic sense to maintain a resource of UK farmland capable of growing a significant proportion and range of our food, whilst also sustaining adequate numbers of people trained in farming skills.

This is particularly the case given the probable future impact of China on the world's potential food supplies. The time is becoming ever closer when China can no longer satisfy its growing population and their changing diet, and this will put even greater pressure on world food supplies.

In view of all this, has our government understood the enormity of the food crunch heading our way? Do they have an adequate strategic plan? Recent experiences - such as the collapse of the financial markets and the consequent credit crunch - leave little grounds for optimism on this score. This is what makes campaigning on these issues all the more important. And it is why the Soil Association's main campaign efforts are directed at achieving 'A Secure Food Future - Organic by 2050'.

The Soil Association's fuller report on these issues, An Inconvenient Truth about our food - neither secure, nor resilient *is available at http://www.soilassociation.org/.*

Frames and conjunctures in present-day capitalism

Karel Williams

The complementary concepts of conjuncture and frame make recent events easier to understand.

―――

'It's awful - why did nobody see it coming?' That was the Queen's sharp question about the financial crisis to the assembled social scientists at the opening of the LSE's new academic building in November 2008. Those of us with negative views of hereditary monarchy and the House of Windsor must respect the present Queen, who is no intellectual but has more grip and good sense than most of the salaried intelligentsia. If the Queen had been less polite she might have asked 'what good are social scientists anyway?', because the current financial crisis once again reminds us that many of the knowledges of social science are irrelevant or perniciously pro-cyclical, in that they encourage the upswing and do not anticipate crisis or downturn.

There are of course many reasons for the current financial crisis. It is immediately and technically the result of a failure of regulation to engage with or control long chains of securitisation transactions whose macro result was what Roubini and others have termed the 'shadow banking system'. But we also need to ask how and why this was allowed to happen, especially in the USA, which has a tradition of tough financial regulation. One of the key preconditions of regulatory failure was the chorus of reassurance after the crisis of 2000 from mainstream finance theorists; they presented securitisation and the 'originate and distribute' model of lending as

Frames and conjunctures in present-day capitalism

a process of marketising risk which rendered the illiquid liquid, and incidentally dispersed risk in ways which strengthened the global financial system. On these points, the speeches of bankers such as Ben Bernanke of the US Fed simply echoed the prevailing academic orthodoxy of the 2000s.

This is not the first such misjudgement by social sciences in recent times. In the second half of the 1990s a completely different and much more socio-cultural group of researchers promoted all kinds of misunderstandings about the so called 'new economy' and thereby encouraged the dot.com boom, which ended sharply in 2000 with the tech stock crash. According to the 1990s 'weightless economy' narrative of academics and consultants, the falling costs of (digital) information unglued supply chains and undermined established business models, so that incumbent firms and established suppliers could be unseated by digital start-ups that were to be valued on their prospects rather than their current turnover or profitability. In a longer perspective one could add other misjudgements, especially those of the mainstream economists who supported monetarism in the 1970s and financial deregulation in the 1980s.

In all these cases, social scientists relate to the innovations and enthusiasms of capitalism in much the same way as bishops blessing battleships. Every decade or so another group of social scientists looks out of the windows of their high tower at what the managers and financial intermediaries say they are doing, and what the politicians are promising to do, and then encourages the practitioners to just go ahead and do it, by rationalising current developments as the purpose and achievement of capitalism. The groups of social scientists are different each time, and their techniques and epistemologies range from positivistic algebra to social constructionism. But their effects are much the same, as each new group of critical social scientists promises critical independence and delivers endorsement and legitimation of the emerging nonsense of each new age. A cynic might conclude that the end result is pro-cyclical social science: social scientific attempts to understand capitalism unintentionally produce knowledges which make capitalist fluctuations worse.

So it is important to ask why these misjudgements occur - and how we might avoid them in future. One recurrent intellectual cause is the tendency of many different groups of social scientists to confuse the epochal with the conjunctural; they have a tendency to present cartoon histories of historical change from before to after, and misrepresent cyclical developments and temporary values as a kind of permanent new order. This new order is then welcomed as inaugurating an era in which the old economic rules no longer apply.

Sometimes such discursive understandings have performative effects. After the Netscape initial public offering, dot.coms in the late 1990s could be valued highly even if they had no saleable product or business mode. Similarly, private equity partners could deliver high returns after 2000 because they could borrow at low risk premiums as they bought, sold and refinanced firms at ever higher price/earnings multiples. But in both cases these results were the consequence of temporary flows of funds, and the sectoral business model for tech start-ups and leveraged buy-outs was undermined when the flow of funds dried up. However, the intellectual model in itself had led to results that at first appeared to confirm the validity of its arguments.

Our argument is that social sciences could avoid some gross confusions, and maybe achieve a bit more prescience, if they added the concept of conjuncture to their repertoire. Or, more exactly, it would be helpful to distinguish between a semi-permanent frame around economic activity and the more transitory conjunctural ordering of the economy in specific configurations for periods of four to seven years; and to recognise that such conjunctures combine asset values and flows of funds with justifying narratives - which social scientists have often bought into or actively propagated, without properly distinguishing between discourse and practice.

Our aim here is to take up this task of adding conjunctural analysis, through two main sections of argument, which separately analyse frame and conjuncture. These two concepts are complementary: we have no wish to endorse an over-eager revisionism which bends the stick too far and argues that a concept of conjuncture is the only key to understanding present-day capitalism.

Frame: coupon pool capitalism

Epochalism is always mistaken but often tempting, because many things do stay the same for thirty to fifty years, and this feels like a long time in relation to a working or investing life. However such periods are too short to be described as epochs, however that may be defined; the idea of an epoch may be useful in geology or cosmology, but its metaphorical application to socio-economic objects and structures

Frames and conjunctures in present-day capitalism

is seriously confusing. We can sidestep these confusions by proposing the concept of a frame around economic activity, which is enduring but not epochal, because frames do change every few decades. This point emerges very clearly if we consider how mass financialisation in present-day capitalism from the late 1970s onwards is different from the earlier rentier form of financialised capitalism from 1910 to 1940 - which was variously analysed by marxists, liberals and social democrats, from Hilferding and Hobson to Tawney and Keynes.

The earlier rentier capitalism of the 1920s and 1930s was distinguished by the way in which it gave banks and insurance companies an organising role through interlocking directorates, and confined investment to an upper-class minority or rentier stratum, whose calculations and interests were different from those of the unpropertied wage-earning masses. All this changed after the 1970s, in the new frame of what we have termed coupon pool capitalism, where banks increasingly acquired new roles as wholesale traders and as retail marketeers of financial products with the masses, integrated through savings and loans. The new frame became immediately different in three respects after the later 1980s, because there was a 'massification' of household savings; a dramatic growth in the importance of financial intermediaries; and a number of feedback effects on the calculations of firms and households.

First, in contrast with earlier frames, there is now a much wider and probably irreversible spread of coupon ownership, as households in the top half of the income distribution provide feedstock for the financial markets, both by directing savings into a coupon pool through a variety of funds and channels, and by purchasing products, including loans, that generate coupons via securitisation. The combination of mass savings and unrestrained innovation has resulted in a growth in the number and types of coupons traded, and in the employment of intermediaries who manage financial stocks and flows. Whereas earlier upper-middle-class investors were passive owners, 40-50 per cent of current investors are now virtual owners of significant portfolios - themselves silent, but represented by financial intermediaries who speak for the 'shareholder' and claim to understand risk and return. Within this frame, 'personal finance' discourses of financial prudence, risk management and individualised responsibility and opportunity have the task of formatting the savings and borrowing behaviour of the financialised masses.

Second, again in contrast with earlier frames, this is a period of huge opportunity for fee-earning and deal-driven intermediaries, whose leading elements now work for themselves on profit shares in banks, or as venture capitalists, private equity partners and hedge fund managers incentivised on '2 and 20' fee structures (see Adam Leaver in *Soundings* 41). The intermediaries are not a class in themselves with a coherent agenda, but a distributional coalition of individuals and groups whose numbers are increased by the probably irreversible rise of retail mass marketing and wholesale derivatives trading. The retail banking sector is everywhere reconfigured as the mass marketer of savings and loan products, and this makes financial services the first or second largest sector on most national stock exchanges; while innovation around new derivative products after the breakdown of Bretton Woods and the introduction of securitisation has hugely increased dealing volumes in the wholesale markets. Deregulation and technology have contributed to financial innovation at wholesale and retail levels, so that there are now many more different kinds of coupons, some of which are traded in massive volumes to lever profits from small margins, or to generate fee income. While the intermediaries in different ways manage, deploy and trade the funds of the financialised masses, it is also the case that intermediary activities are more than simply delegated management and associated services, since finance increasingly feeds finance in creating new opportunities for fees, trades and margins.

In the third contrast with earlier frames, productive firms are now generally defined as blocks of tradable assets and bundles of operating cash flows, with dealing never far away, as point concepts of value crystallisation become as or more important than stream concepts of value creation. The earlier practices of the Victorian company promoter, the Edwardian financier and the acquisitive conglomerate CEO are now generalised, when public companies (financial and non-financial) are threatened with takeover or loss of support from their institutional shareholders if they do not defensively restructure themselves. The practices of 'everything for sale' are also pressed into new areas, including the German Mittelstand (the small and medium sized family-owned German companies that were for a long time seen as the backbone of the German economy). As well as being the virtual owners of coupons, often on an intermediated basis, the financialised masses are active house capitalists, with 50 to 70 per cent of households directly enrolled as home-owners, even before the rise of interest-only mortgages and buy-to-let as a form of savings in many national economies.

Frames and conjunctures in present-day capitalism

It is tempting to insert these striking developments into traditional theorisations about before and after epochal change, or national varieties of capitalism resting on new institutional complementarities. In this case, coupon pool capitalism would be represented as an epochal new stage of capitalism which inverts previous system characteristics; or it would be represented as a new national variety of capitalism spreading from its original Anglo-American base. In our view, both positions would be wrong, because the developments outlined above do not work by establishing system-wide behavioural coherence or institutional complementarity of the old-fashioned kind, and the coupon pool is not a regulatory institution. Equally important, such developments do not inaugurate a 'disorganised capitalism' because, as we argue below, successive conjunctures do represent temporarily organised spaces. From this point of view, the coupon pool frame (without conjunctural analysis) is an incomplete answer to questions about structuration and outcomes.

Conjuncture

The conjuncture is the space of temporary, contradictory and partial organisation, which we define in a Braudelesque, non-Marxist, sense. A conjuncture is simply the distinctive combination of circumstances within which events and episodes happen for periods which typically last from four to seven years. This combination mixes two sets of hard and soft defining characteristics. The hard economic aspect of conjuncture comes from a capital market configuration of asset prices and the availability of funds, which is embedded in mass saving and consumption patterns as well as trade imbalances. The soft socio-cultural support is supplied by appropriate grand narratives produced and circulated by practitioners, consultants and the commentariat in the media, as well as academics, all variously rationalising the trajectory. In these terms, the New Economy period from 1996 to 2000, or the excess liquidity period from 2000 to 2007, were both distinct and successive conjunctures.

All this can be illustrated with a brief description of the excess liquidity conjuncture. This developed out of the wreck of the new economy after 2000, when the tech stock crash led to a two year fall in the public markets and then their subsequent rise. Rising asset prices were encouraged by three separate accelerators: first, low interest rates adopted in the USA as a counter-cyclical measure after the tech stock crash; second, unregulated credit creation as the innovation of securitisation allowed banks to lend and lend again without balance sheet constraint; third, global patterns of trade imbalance and international differences in appetite for savings and loans that fuelled the flow - Asian manufacturers and all kinds of commodity producers were remitting funds to the major financial centres in New York and London, which were also pushing and recycling loans until sub-prime mortgages went wrong.

The conjuncture from 2000 to 2007 took a cyclical form, and ended as most capitalist credit cycles do with a failure of liquidity that left the over-borrowed holding depreciating assets, which created a crisis of solvency; and in this case the crisis affected ordinary home-owners as well as intermediary players in the market. But this is not the kind of recurrent cycle envisaged by political economists who rest cyclicality on behavioural universals such as the shallow judgement of investors in liquid markets (Keynes) or the conventional nature of bank lending (Minsky). Each conjuncture is different, because it is animated by a new story. In the post-2000 case, rhetorics about alternative asset classes and new investment strategies provided favourable discursive conditions for the growth of hedge funds and private equity, which each fed off cheap debt; while the general alibi about the 'marketisation of risk' rationalised and informed the securitisation activities of investment bankers, who developed a new business model of proprietary trading.

A conjuncture temporarily aligns narrative and numbers as long as the returns generated in the market validate the stories which rationalise the money-making. And, under these specific conditions, Minsky is correct about the difference between financialised asset markets and ordinary commodified product markets: in financialised asset markets with a strong justifying narrative, an increase in asset prices will induce increased demand. At this point, financial intermediaries will carry on doing the same deals and trades until discrepancies outside their models and experience overwhelm their money-making and impose a fundamental rethink of their modus operandi. Unsound fundamentals and impending crashes are irrelevant for most elite intermediaries, whose mentality in 2007 was summed up by the Citigroup CEO Chuck Prince just before the credit crunch: 'as long as the music is playing, you've got to get up and dance. We're still dancing' (*Financial Times*, 9.7.07).

If we relate all this to established academic views of capitalism, the point

Frames and conjunctures in present-day capitalism

about conjuncture is that things do fit together, but with more difficulty and for only a while. Part of the problem is the discrepancies and contradictions within conjunctures, which are only self-fulfilling up to a point. But the question about outcomes and dynamics is also complicated by the fact that the values and relations which concern us, in frame and conjuncture, do not establish a logic that excludes all others. To begin with, many of the new effects are connected with capital flows and asset prices, but these variables are only indirectly connected to earned income (insofar as conjunctural change generates more or less employment). Income from current employment remains primary for most households: even after including pensioners, more than 80 per cent of the income in the middle three UK income quintiles is earned income from employment. Thus macro economic and monetary effects arising from changed employment relations, international wage differences and so on remain important.

In our view, coupon pool capitalism is marked by internal contradictions and multiple discrepancies which have no single source. That position distinguishes us from Marxisant analysts like David Harvey or Robert Brenner, who still believe in a law of value. But this was elegantly destroyed in Cutler's 1979 essay which argued that a general law of value (Marxist or marginalist) cannot operate in any existing economy where different economic subjects operate in various calculative frames and under different accounting regulations for recognising profits.

The frame does create new dynamics, because the stability of coupon pool capitalism does require some balancing of labour, product and capital market demands. Leaving narrative complications aside, this balance is inherently problematic, because competitive product markets frustrate the delivery of value through earnings, while liquid financial markets are destabilised by speculation and swings in sentiment. Much value is then unstably created and lost through reversible flows of funds which inflate and deflate asset price bubbles. Wholesale markets add further instabilities, because financial innovators have no property rights and cannot prevent rapid imitation and erosion of profit margins, so that dealing profits have to be augmented by high velocity trading or by leveraging positions with borrowed funds, which magnifies the consequences of speculation.

The major actors in coupon pool capitalism need a story and also have to put on a performance, because everybody knows that talk is cheap in the new polity, where intermediary elites must endlessly rehearse the justification of their positions and tax privileges in terms of general socio-economic benefits. Thus private equity has to sell itself as a better form of ownership than the public company, while hedge funds emphasise the market benefits of hedging by players who do more than take long-only positions. The financialised masses may be virtual owners, but they are also voters, whose political support for funded saving and light-touch regulation of financial services cannot be entirely taken for granted, however strongly the discourses of 'personal finance' interpellate the subject.

Prescience (not prediction)

So what is gained by recognising conjuncture, and the roundabout repercussions of the discrepancies within and between narrative and numbers? It helps us to understand how and why coupon pool capitalism is inherently unstable, and can generate such different outcomes in two successive conjunctures. Everything changes with the conjuncture, except perhaps for the one general tendency towards elite enrichment and upwards redistribution, which continues because in each new conjuncture a changing group of elite intermediaries is well-placed to act as a distributional coalition, skimming value from revenue flows and asset trading. It is not possible, of course, to predict the timing of inflections and changes of conjuncture. At least, until we understand much more about the sudden collapse of fragile beliefs, all we can say is that regularities and outcomes persist until they break down. But it should be possible to acquire more prescience about the direction of effects, and the different risks and uncertainties which the masses face, in each new conjuncture.

Four poems

—

The poetry in this issue comes from *Poetry Review*, which was one hundred years old in May. For today's reader this doesn't just mean a terrific literary 'back-story'. The weight of past 'greats', from Hardy and Eliot to Ginsberg and Beckett, Larkin and Berger, generates a kind of momentum - which we celebrate in the *A Century of Poetry Review*, which will be published by Carcanet in October. The *Review* may be a hefty vehicle to steer, but its role as what the *Guardian* calls poetry's 'magazine of record' means that it remains the periodical most poets want to appear in, and to read. Functioning as a kind of build-your-own encyclopaedia, it's shaping the canon of the future.

So *PR* affords a sort of short-cut for anyone interested in poetry, but perhaps lacking time or inclination for detailed study. It's a way to access a vibrant part of contemporary culture. But the magazine, and the work it publishes, are of course more than that. *Poetry Review* understands that poetry may be many things to many people: samizdat semaphore, cultural debate, the expression of a variety of voices or, perhaps above all, a form which allows the exploration of major moral, political and epistemological questions. Recent issues, for example, have focused on the risks and gains of politicised culture and on the new eco-poetics. Moreover, since it is neither necessarily fiction, nor as answer-led as the essay, the poem can 'tell the whole truth but tell it slant', as Emily Dickinson has it. In doing so it can show the reader how to *make sense* for him- or herself of the range of often-highly-determined texts with which contemporary culture surround us.

Though these poems are taken from a recent issue (98:4, *The Ghost in the Machine*), they are representative, in their seriousness and range, of the magazine as a whole (even though, naturally, we have a spread of gender and cultures in every issue).

Fiona Sampson poetryreview@poetrysociety.org.uk

Night of love

Ingeborg Bachmann

Translated by Michael Lyons and Patrick Drysdale

In a night of love after a long night

I have learnt to speak again and I wept

because a word came out of me. I have again learnt to walk,

walked up to the window and said hunger and light

and night was fine by me for light.

After an overlong night

slept peacefully again,

trusting in this,

I spoke more easily in the dark,

spoke on through the day,

ran my fingers over my face,

I am no longer dead.

A bush, from which fire struck in the night.

My avenger stepped out and called himself life.

I even said: let me die, and meant

without fear my more cherished death.

(from *Ich weiss keine bessere Welt* © Piper Verlag 2000)

Four poems

Poppy day

John Burnside

The butcher arrives with a love song

he learned from his father.

Out on the kill floor, veiled in a butterslick

circumflex of marrowfat and bone,

he rinses off the knife and goes to work,

his voice so sweet, the children come to hear

the beauty of it, slipped between a vein

and what the veal calf thought would last

forever.

  Barely a shudder rises through the hand

that holds the blade

      and yet he guides it down

so gently, it falls open, like a flower.

And still the children come, to hear him sing,

his voice so soft, it's no more than a whisper.

The note produced

Paul Farley

The sixty-four foot organ pipe,

the low C, shuddering Jesus Christ,

the engine room that makes cathedrals

dive, dive, dive, fathoms of flue

that drill into the bedrock, shift

knuckles and long bones in the crypt,

and you can feel the bottom line

right where the ribs all congregate,

a shiver trapped and brought to life.

Four poems

Sand tale

John Kinsella

> *covering all*
>> - Tracy Ryan

Tracy and I are less than two years apart in age.

We have similar but different life experiences of growing up.

We both emerged in the same corner of the world.

I did high school in the country, she did a bit of primary school

in the country. We both spent a lot of time in Perth

when Perth was different. She was from a suburb

bordering the hills, I was from an inner southern river

suburb that bordered hundreds and hundreds

and hundreds of acres of bush, as well

as a swampy limb of the river

that became a creek. Old Bateman's farm

was down there, and cows got stuck

in the silty riverflats. Tracy spent

most of her time in her suburb,

I spent a lot of my time

out of the city. At the farm,

or maybe north to see my father. Sand

was big in the city but rare on the farm. Red-brown dirt

up there. Not sand that'd pour through your fingers.

Not sand that was black and let water run

Soundings

through like there was no end to the earth.

Not sand that was yellow as if it had been dyed,

sickly and sweet at once. It would set rock hard.

Being hit by a rock of that could break your skull.

Not white sand that would grow nothing

but looked and felt so clean. Sandpits.

Pleasure. Fetish. Exhuming the lost,

lifted out as easily slipped in and away.

Hungry, but ready to give it up. Brought in

from the beaches: the thin river beaches

in need of topping up. At night, early in the morning,

shovel and sacks, robbing the public,

the behest, the dyadic self.

The flat discs of jellyfish: moon translucent,

never quiet: you see nothing but sand caked on their

eating parts. Or the spotted mottled brown

jellyfish with its bunched-up, thick

tentacles, cloying beads of sand. That's what

comes of endosymbionts, tossed up in their armadas.

Their multiplicity is sandlike and yet

we draw few analogies from it. Like brown jellyfish

in the hourglass. As if humour is everything

in childhood, and we're not serious and bleak

drying on the sand, digging so it will collapse,

so it will give way. The edifices to be knocked down,

Four poems

eaten by breeze and slight tidal shift of the river.

Though in winter the jetties gulp for breath,

sand in cracks floats out. Sand of the river,

slowly making its way down

to the river mouth. Sand that sets

when you come out of the murky

river, a Swan River Whaler sighting,

and all your tension about swimming lessons

sets as a new skin that dries and cracks and even

peels away. That sand too. But there was no

real sand up at the farm. If it poured

it was as dust, up there, in the valley. Clouds

that swarmed and rolled and choked.

The fine film that covered

like a lyrical aftertaste. Gritted your eyes,

but you didn't need to pick the grains out,

finer, it wept away. But where

I went to school in Geraldton - coastal town

where sand plains are farmed against the lack of rain,

where you travel inland to search out the stony country

of the next people, the Yamaji elder telling his mate

that he's crossing over just about now,

on the road to Mount Magnet.

POETRY REVIEW

Discover the best of contemporary poetry

Poetry Review is the Poetry Society's acclaimed quarterly magazine, packed with the very best in international and British poetry. Its Centrefold section explores issues such as ecology, materialism and political culture; the magazine also includes scholarly reviews of recent collections.

The summer issue of *Poetry Review*, Cosmopolis, will take a look at everything from French sound-poetry to the Balkan Haiku, and the contemporary scene in Iceland. There are also new poems from Wendy Cope, Jo Shapcott, Matthew Sweeney, Daljit Nagra and John Burnside writing on the controversial topic of improvisation.

Make sure you don't miss the summer – or any other issue of Poetry Review – take out a subscription now.

Poetry Review subscription (four issues) ● *UK £30* ● *Overseas £40*

THE POETRY SOCIETY

To subscribe, call +44 (0)20 7420 9880
email: membership@poetrysociety.org.uk
www.poetrysociety.org.uk

The millennial generation and politics

Ben Little

The challenge of the ipod generation to politics.

———

J oss Garman, one of the founders of anti-airport expansion group Plane Stupid, recently laid down the gauntlet to the secretary of state for energy and climate change: 'It's time for Ed Miliband to decide which generation he is with. Ours, or Brown's' (*Guardian*, Comment is Free, March 2009). Garman framed the challenge of climate change as the battle of the Millennial Generation against the baby boomers. His argument is that - unlike previous protest movements - climate change activism is not a phase or a fad, but the result of a genuine difference of interest between generations:

> This isn't about being disaffected and rebellious without a cause. This isn't about dropping out, rejecting the norm, culture jamming and hacking the system. This isn't even about altruism. It's not just about defending the rights and lives of those who are less fortunate than us, and it certainly isn't about polar bears. This is about us. For the millennial generation the patronising clichés fall apart, because this isn't about ideals so much as hard science and the terrifying reality that what the scientists have been warning us all about for years - those sea level rises, catastrophic droughts and melting ice caps - will now happen in our lifetimes.

He is right; the priorities of those entering their thirties over the next ten years must be very different from those that reached the same age in the 1980s, or even the 1990s. Without a doubt climate change is the most pressing issue, but we can also add to the list of complaints of my age group the challenge of an increasingly unequal society, astronomic levels of personal and national debt and an aggressive foreign policy that destabilises the world we are inheriting.

The problem with Garman's argument, however, is his claim that as a group we are somehow up for this challenge. Citing Eric Greenberg and Karl Weber's *Generation We* (Pachatusan 2008), he suggests that behind Plane Stupid's airport protests there is a whole generation standing by to join in. There is not. Not yet at least. On the contrary, most research shows that in the UK young people are increasingly disengaged from most kinds of political or community activities and lack the means or the will to take on our parents' generation in a collective way.

Greenberg and Weber claim that the millennials are 'history's most active volunteering generation', and propose the idea that 'Generation We' is one that rejects old political allegiances and is collectively building a progressive, fair society through a paradigm shift in community participation - a wonderful vision for the future, but one firmly situated in the USA. Their argument may have resonance in North America, but it seems that the opposite is the case in the UK. The 2004 Euyoupart survey indicated that outside of sports clubs very few 15-25 year olds volunteer at all. Only 1 per cent had ever volunteered for an environmental organisation (such as Plane Stupid) - the same proportion as for animal rights groups - and the highest level of participation was with charities, at a mere 3 per cent. The idea that young people are rejecting mainstream politics in favour of volunteering and activism is simply not true, although the disconnection from formal democracy remains accurate.

A majority (76 per cent) of young people think politics are important, but only 24 per cent said they actually had an interest in it, a terrifyingly low figure, but still higher than the percentage that were volunteering. Levels of ignorance are also significant, with 41 per cent not knowing the difference between left- and right-wing politics. Ignorance leads to inaction: 68 per cent of eligible 18-25 year olds never actually use their vote, by far the lowest participation of any age group in the UK. British youth's engagement with politics and the social realm ranked among the worst in Europe, with equivalent age groups demonstrating less interest in public life only in Slovakia and Estonia.[1]

The millennial generation and politics

These findings are in line with a 2002 report by the electoral commission, and are also supported by more recent qualitative analysis conducted by Ipsos-Mori and Reform. While the latter is more positive about the possibilities of what they call Britain's IPODs, the focus groups project a picture of a whole generation that lacks the will, the knowledge or the enthusiasm to actively take a stake in their society.[2] There is an argument that this disengagement is just a normal part of being young, but this may be to underestimate the problem. Alison Park argued in 2000, of the age cohort born in the late 1970s and early 1980s, that it would take a great deal of catching up to overcome the 'democratic deficit' from which that cohort suffered, and become comparable to the 30-year-olds of that time.[3] Nine years after this was written there is little to indicate that we have.

Britain's 'IPODs' and America's 'Wes': Boris and Barack

Barack Obama's success in courting a younger vote is well documented. Even in the primaries his appeal to America's Generation We was impressive. In some states there was a 330 per cent increase in turn out among 18 to 29 year olds. Likewise, Boris Johnson's victory in the London 2008 mayoral election was built on a voting alliance of the disengaged IPOD generation and traditionally conservative older voters.

At first glance there are similarities between these two campaigns, though they come from opposite ends of the political spectrum. Much has been made of the way both used the internet and particularly Facebook. Both politicians came into office on the promise of change to the status quo. Both ran largely positive campaigns - although this was made significantly easier for Johnson by the vituperous attacks on Livingstone appearing daily in London's *Evening Standard*. It would be easy to conclude from this that the key to engaging the young is to be different, use new technologies to catch their attention and 'be nice'. However this simple position is not borne out by further analysis. While there were some similarities in the manner in which each candidate appealed to a younger demographic, the reasons for the support they received differ markedly. Although Obama represented a paradigm shift in the American political landscape, a vote for Johnson offered an opportunity to lampoon British politics. Many of the Boris voters I have met saw a vote for him as a way of giving organised politics the finger. This manifested itself in three main statements (paraphrasing):

Soundings

I'd much rather read about Boris in the papers every day.
Anything is better than that ideologue Ken.
Of course it'd be ridiculous if Boris won, that's why I'm voting for him.
It's not like he can take us to war or anything.

Thus, unlike voting for Obama, which was a statement of faith in, and renewal of American politics, voting for Johnson was partly a statement of discontent. Despite a grudging respect for Livingstone's values, many resented what they saw as his inflexibility and dogmatism; Johnson, on the other hand, appeared to stand for nothing more than a parody of eccentric Englishness.

A large part of the mindset was that if we had to be subjected to the denigrated spectacle of party politics in the media, at least someone like Johnson would make it more entertaining. In the absence of any real awareness of what the mayor does (beyond the congestion charge), the thinking behind a vote for Johnson was that the most significant thing that a mayor offered London was an identity, and Johnson seemed to offer the intangible trait of 'fun'.

Nevertheless, the willingness of the 18-25 year olds to vote in the London election is significant, regardless of the rationale (or the result): participation in local elections could be one of the key ways to rebuild political consciousness. But for this to happen there needs to be a major shift both in the culture of community/social participation in the UK, and quite possibly in our electoral system. One key aspect of the youth support attracted by Obama - as was not the case for those supporting Johnson - was the willingness of young Americans to go out and campaign on behalf of their candidate. Obama did not just re-engage young people with politics: his campaign turned a generation of volunteers into a generation of political activists.

While there are definite similarities in terms of lifestyle and interest, the gap in social and political activism between Generation We in the USA and the IPOD generation in the UK appears to be consistent with this observation. Although both groups share a disaffection with party politics, the same cannot be said for their levels of community participation. One statistic claims that a staggering 83 per cent of Generation We volunteered in their last year of school. This puts into perspective the roughly 24 per cent of IPODs who did the same (and this is including participation in sports clubs). However, Americans are not intrinsically more community-minded; there are definite reasons for this discrepancy - and they are cultural and institutional.

The main factor is the admissions policy of most American higher education establishments, which, modelled on that of the Ivy League universities, weights academic ability alongside sporting achievement, personality and the all important 'extra-curricular' activities. This approach emerged in the first half of the twentieth century, after purely academic selection had led to what was considered - at Harvard particularly - a disproportionate number of New York Jews being admitted.[4] Over and above outright anti-semitism, the university saw its actions as helping to safeguard its income from the 'old money' east coast families, who have a long tradition of financial support for their alma maters. The system continues to this day. The Harvard website warns applicants in the following way:

> Academic accomplishment in high school is important, but the Admissions Committee also considers many other criteria, such as community involvement, leadership and distinction in extracurricular activities, and work experience.

Similarly other, non-Ivy league universities such as UCLA (which produced the 83 per cent statistic cited by Greenberg and Weber) require their students to have: 'Extensive leadership and initiative in school and/or community organizations and activities' (see, for example, the UCLA website).

This emphasis on community participation is for the most part an American idiosyncrasy. While the importance of the personal statement cannot be downplayed in the UK, Cambridge University, for example, makes no reference to community participation in its application requirements. Elite universities in Britain instead seek further academic distinction for the selection of their students, as evidenced, for instance, in their campaign for the new A* grade at A-Level. In contrast, in the USA community involvement is not simply a worthwhile activity; it is an assessable part of a rounded education. As such, not only must young people proactively participate in their communities, they must distinguish themselves in doing so, particularly if they want to gain admittance to the top universities. To support these endeavours, there is a whole infrastructure to facilitate volunteering, with funding for projects, and pressure from schools and parents to 'succeed' as community-minded individuals.

In short, despite its racist origins, this requirement for community involvement is the reason that America has a larger, more integrated, third sector than the UK. The sector is better funded, has more volunteers and lacks the sneery 'do-gooder' response that characterises the typical attitude to social participation in this country. When community groups approach their elected officials they are taken seriously. And this means that when a politician like Obama emerges, the skills and experience that people have gained in the competition for a university place can be transferred to the political arena. This is also the reason that 'grass-roots' politics in the USA is an effective way of mobilising and building support, while in the UK its invocation is often simply rhetorical.

Promoting activism and engagement in the UK

The implications of a generation adrift from politics have not been lost on the British government. A substantial majority of the funds allocated to volunteering in general have been diverted specifically to the young, with the strict target of creating one million more volunteers. For the past two years I have been teaching on a module for first year media students in which they have to organise and run a social campaign as part of their assessment. This year the students have been the beneficiaries of some of these government funds, administered through the charity Junction49. The results have been impressive, and have led to a vast increase in the scope and potential of the projects available for students.

That said, even with this added support the students' campaigns started tentatively; only one group began their semester of action with any clear idea of what they would do and how they would achieve it. Most struggled with the idea of how to make connections to other people, to institutions and to government. They had been taught across a variety of themes during the previous semester, but - while they could articulate why child protection or global warming were important issues - even after taught sessions on campaigning many lacked the mindset to understand how they could effect change personally.

On a hunch that more students would respond to the participatory, media-orientated sensibilities of direct-action-type groups than to more traditional campaigning, I invited two speakers from this kind of campaign to address the students - Richard, a veteran airport protestor from Plane Stupid, and Robin, a

The millennial generation and politics

founding member of Space Hijackers. The central tenet of direct action, born from the very lack of faith in the parliamentary process that characterises the IPOD generation, is that you can intervene as an individual or small group to oppose or counter-act most forms of injustice. It just takes imagination, guts and a bit of planning.

Both Plane Stupid and Space Hijackers have been able not only to make activism 'fun', but also to create effective interventions. For example Robin described a protest against fashion label Box Fresh's use of Zapatista imagery in a line of clothing. In this action the activists dressed as Zapatistas and stood outside the flagship shop in Covent Garden chanting and distributing fliers. Within a few hours they had an agreement from the shop to donate profits from the clothing line to a Mexican NGO, and to provide information about the Zapatistas' struggle alongside the merchandise in the shop. The same group had also garnered media attention for the 2007 arms exhibition in the Excel Centre by driving a tank up to the front doors and pretending to auction it to the highest bidder.

The Space Hijackers intervention model is based on a politics of individual action in a globalised context. Their combination of performance and politics seems productive, even if their basic philosophy is shared by the HSBC marketing department ('Think global, act local'). At the national level, for them the state figures purely as an oppressive apparatus - the paymasters of the police whose job it is to disrupt their peaceful but ostentatious events. The government, then, is less a target and more a facilitator for other global actors, such as arms companies, banks and fashion labels, who control and propagate what the Hijackers see as an exploitative, violent, consumerist form of globalisation.

This complete lack of faith in Westminster politics then manifests itself as a huge gap in their political activities. The local is important and can be linked to global issues, but there is little in between except cynicism. Some of the best work my students did reflected these values, as did their anonymous responses towards the end of the course to the question 'What is Politics?', where comments like: 'trying to fix up what sleazebag politicians do' were common. Perhaps I should have put more emphasis on the positive role that democratic participation can have, but I think that mindset is so entrenched that to convince a majority of the students that their votes are important would have been a bit like herding cats (I'll work on it next year though).

Soundings

The emphasis on the local could be seen in the number of student campaigns that focused either on campus or, in the case of students based locally, on their immediate neighbourhoods. Examples included the Sexual Hijackers, who stormed university events dressed in multi-coloured fluorescent tutus to distribute condoms and literature on STDs, and Stand Up, a talent contest and club night that raised money for anti-gang charities and invited speakers to raise awareness of the impact of gun and knife crime. Where groups attempted to deal with more global issues, they did so in a way that was again focused on the local community. A reusable shopping bag painting session was organised on campus, and another group set up a swap shop, both campaigns aimed at countering consumerism as a driver of global warming.

A few groups stepped outside this comfort zone. Two are worth mentioning. The first, inspired by the tactics of the Space Hijackers, organised a 'clean-in' in parliament square to protest against poverty wages in the capital. The shock for them was, firstly, that it was so easy to organise and, secondly, that the police were so accommodating. In the end, while they cleaned the barriers put up for them by the government that was the target of their campaign, I spent my time in conversation with their assigned police team, trying to convince them that the Plane Stupid protest on the roof of parliament was not just a stunt, but an effective way of getting the media to take the debate on airport expansion seriously.

The second group were working at the council level to campaign for more legal graffiti walls. In complete contrast to the response to the 'clean-in' group from central government, these students' requests for information about their policies on the issue from seven different councils were met with stony silence from all but one. The seventh, Barnet, stopped responding when they found out that the students were running a campaign to encourage them to change their policy. They subsequently shifted their tactic to make contact with individual councillors, but I am yet to find out how they got on with this.

The complete contrast in the experience the two groups had of their interactions with government is indicative of the vast gulf that exists between national and local levels of bureaucracy, not in their commitment to public service, but in the amount of investment and resources that are allocated to encouraging active citizenship. If the government wants to harness the enthusiasm and energy of the generation that my students and I belong to, they have their priorities back to front. Throwing money at youth volunteering, or Gordon Brown's latest initiative that proposes 50

The millennial generation and politics

hours of compulsory community service by the age of 19, will only be effective if the projects are administered at a local level, rather than through central targets that make good manifesto pledges.

If in the future political parties (and particularly the left) want to be able to rely on the mass support of my generation, they will need to make note of three things. First, that grass-roots politics is always a genuinely local affair, and that for that to happen there needs to be a genuine local democracy to participate in, one that can set its own targets and priorities. Devolution and a mayor for London has been a good start, but there needs to be more. This was the key message of the *Power to The People* report into the state of British democracy in 2005, and politicians would do well to heed it. If, in Britain, we want a figure that inspires the same level of grass-roots support as Barack Obama, local politics and community participation will first need to be reinvigorated.

Secondly, this generation does believe in abstract ideals such as fairness and social justice, but they will reject anything that has the whiff of dogma. The notion of wedding yourself overtly to an ideology died as a mainstream concept in the USA in the 1950s, and it died in the UK in the 1980s, as British and American culture became what John Dumbrell calls 'a distinct culture area'.[5] There is no need for the left to return to such positions, however; its aims can be achieved in other ways.

Thirdly, there is no harm in making politics fun; in fact it encourages participation and reduces the intrinsically confrontational nature of many political disagreements. The G20 protests in central London were a case in point: the carnivalesque approach taken by the two main alliances meant that what was billed as a riot was, for the most part, an event carried off with a friendly party atmosphere that stilled managed to communicate dissent. There is no reason why, in other contexts, participation in politics should not take on the same jovial air.

Finally, I would say to Joss Garman that framing the fight against global warming as a battle of the generations is counter-productive. General elections can be swung in this country by the votes of a few hundred thousand people in key marginals; if just five per cent more of our generation voted it would be enough to make us the king-makers in the next general election. It was enough for Boris Johnson. While direct action is an important part of the mix, another part is using the electoral system to reshape the priorities of government to the values, concerns and struggles that we and future generations will face. Our democracy is a conversation between all the people who live in our society, and if enough of us start talking through our ballot papers, other generations will have no choice but to listen.

I would like to thank Robin Priestly and Richard George for their time and valuable contribution to the thought that went into this piece.

Notes

1. Carolyn Moore and Kerry Longhurst, *Euyoupart: National Report UK*, available at www.sora.at/images/doku/D15UKReport.pdf 2005; and Sora Institute, *Why Participate?*, available at: www.sora.at/images/doku/sora_euyoupart_results.pdf 2005.

2. Sarah Castell, Andrew Haldenby, Lucy Parsons and Oliver Sweet, *A New Reality: Government and The IPOD Generation*, Ipsos-Mori and Reform, available at www.ipsos-mori.com/_assets/pdfs/ipod%20generation%20report%20a4%20v.1.pdf 2008.

3. Alison Park, 'The Generation Game', *British Social Attitudes*, Vol.17, Sage 2000.

4. See www.newyorker.com/archive/2005/10/10/051010crat_atlarge?currentPage=5.

5. John Dumbrell, *A Special Relationship: Anglo-American Relations in the Cold War and After*, Macmillan 2001, p32.

Constructing a left politics

Bryan Gould

It is time to slough off neoliberalism and return to a politics of social justice

———

A s the global economic crisis gathers force, it not only sweeps before it the flotsam of discredited economic doctrines; it also demands a complete reappraisal of how economies and societies work. It poses again the great questions that underlie all political debate, and it poses them in the certain knowledge that the answers given over the past thirty years - and so widely accepted - must now be rejected.

This is, in other words, one of those rare moments when it is not only possible but positively essential to go back to first principles. We must ask again what is the purpose of politics, what is the role of government, does democracy matter, and - for those who see the need and seek the opportunity for reform - what does it mean to be on the left in politics.

Those questions must be asked, of course, at a time when - in Britain at least - left politics has run into the buffers. The concessions and subterfuges that were thought to be necessary to win power and then to hold it are now unmasked not just as craven but as totally destructive of anything that could have been legitimately regarded as the true purpose of left politics. If there is one incontrovertible lesson to be learned, it is that a left politics that is disconnected from principle and analysis will lead to failure and defeat.

The opportunity is, then, to think again about that body of principle and structured analysis that should underpin any left approach to politics. Our starting-point for such an inquiry must surely be a recognition that, since the late 1970s, and with the often unstated acquiescence of the left, the political agenda has been dominated by neoliberal thinking.

The dominance of this self-serving doctrine has been a huge achievement for those who already exercised great economic power, but felt their privilege threatened by the political power of democratic electorates. They feared, correctly, that elected governments, accountable to the widest range of interests, would not tolerate a system which unfairly favoured the rich and powerful by allowing them to rig the contest for power in their favour.

The rise of neoliberal hegemony

The powerful responded to this threat by bringing about changes, around the end of the 1970s, which negated the power of democracy - changes whose significance was hardly recognised at the time. They made elected governments irrelevant, by acquiring a degree of economic power that would allow them to face down and blackmail all but the most powerful democratic governments - and to bend even the most powerful governments to their will, by using their economic power and invulnerability to political pressure.

The individual steps by which this was achieved need be only briefly rehearsed here. One of the earliest of these masqueraded as a purely technical change that would help international trade and investment, and that was sold to the ordinary citizen as a welcome reduction in bureaucracy. That change, of course, was the removal of exchange controls by Reagan and Thatcher so that international capital was free to roam the world in search of the most favourable investment opportunities. In one step, the rules of the game had changed hugely. Investors no longer had to comply with the requirements of elected governments. Instead, governments found themselves played off against each other by investors who commanded greater and greater resources as the now global economy was funnelled into fewer and fewer hands.

It was governments that now had to sue for terms; they would lose out in the competition for investment if they did not comply with the demands of the multinationals. The investors, on the other hand, now understood that they could exercise their power quite irresponsibly. It was, after all, governments - not the

Constructing a left politics

investors - that had to answer to their electorates. The investors answered to no one but their shareholders. And most costs could be 'externalised', or passed on to taxpayers who no longer had a voice. A further consequence was that voters began to understand that their governments could no longer protect them, and confidence in the democratic process began to weaken.

At around the same time, monetarism became the accepted wisdom, on the left as well as the right - the doctrine that managing the economy was a more or less technical exercise in controlling inflation (the only goal, it was said, that mattered) by regulating the price of money. This technical task could safely be entrusted to unaccountable officials - bankers no less - so that, in one simple step, democratic government was excluded from perhaps the central function for which it was elected.

These ground-breaking changes were reinforced by re-shaping political structures in the image of international capital. Multinational investors found it increasingly irksome to have to deal with national governments, each with its own set of requirements, each reflecting the particular interests and priorities of their own voters. They insisted that economies would function more efficiently if those controlling investment capital could deal with authorities (such as the European Union) that matched their own multinational structure and scale - unelected multinational bureaucracies whose goals coincided with their own. So powerful was the momentum towards the integration of national economies in the name of greater economic efficiency that no one seemed to notice that the long-term consequence was not only an actual reduction in economic efficiency but also a political loss of a most serious kind - the replacement of democratic governments as the ultimate authority by multinational capital.

The ability of multinational capital to set the political agenda meant that a doctrine that could never have been directly sold to voters in individual countries became the dominant driver of the world economy - the view that markets are infallible, that they must not be regulated or interfered with in any way, that the interests of shareholders and the bottom line are all that matters, and that governments must step aside while market forces have their way.

Few seem to have understood - not even politicians supposedly of the left - that an 'infallible' market and democracy cannot co-exist. The whole point of democracy, after all, is that ordinary people can use the political power of democratic legitimacy to offset what would otherwise be the overwhelming economic power of the privileged minority. If even democratic politicians accept that they are powerless to intervene in the market, and that it would be literally improper and counter-productive for them to do so, then the powerful are unconstrained in their ability to impose their will on the rest of society.

We can now see the inevitable consequences of that extraordinary concession by democratic politicians - one that is even more incredible when made by politicians of the left. Unrestrained markets will always threaten a conspiracy against the general interest - as indeed Adam Smith pointed out. They will always lead to excesses. They will always, as a consequence, in the end destroy themselves. The global recession was the direct and inevitable consequence.

Power and politics

We can also see how and why the New Labour government lost its way. Its fascination with the rich and powerful, its acceptance that the unregulated market must always prevail, its belief that market solutions will always be best, and its embrace of a global economy dominated by international capital, all meant that it opted out of the role that most of its supporters expected it to fill - the diffusion of power in society so that the less powerful were protected and treated fairly.

Tony Blair seems to have believed that he could take the pain out of politics - and even the politics out of politics. But politics in a democracy is the means by which we resolve issues that would otherwise be settled by less acceptable means; we wouldn't bother with the messy business of politics if it were not preferable to brute force or the victory of the most powerful. And those issues - arising as they do from the ever-present need to allocate scarce resources and to reconcile conflicting interests - cannot be wished away. Their resolution will shape the crucial determinants of how well society functions and how comfortable individuals feel within it.

All politics, in the end, is a response to a fundamental characteristic of social organisation. All societies demonstrate an inevitable tendency for power to concentrate in a few hands. The power may be physical, economic, or social - but at its most fundamental it is power to make choices, the freedom to choose, even at the expense of, and against the interests of, others.

In any society, those who are stronger, cleverer, or luckier, or who enjoy some other advantage, will inevitably acquire more power than others. They will then, with equal inevitability, use that power to enhance their advantage, accreting to themselves differential privileges which will make them yet more powerful, entrenching their advantage and defending it against attack - and by so doing reinforcing the disadvantage of others. The response that should be made to that intensifying concentration of power is the central and defining issue of politics.

The dictator will say that there is nothing wrong with power being concentrated in a few hands, as long as those hands are his. Patrician conservatives argue that it is inevitably a permanent feature of any social organisation, and that the stability it provides is on the whole beneficial: the emphasis should therefore be on making the disparity in power acceptable, by requiring the powerful to exercise their power humanely and with some kind of social conscience - a kind of *noblesse oblige*. On this account, the less powerful will be conditioned by social pressures to accept their inferior lot in life, and the deserved superiority of their betters, through a well-developed social hierarchy. The liberal (or, according to taste, the social democrat or proponent of the 'third way') will also accept that a substantial degree of inequality is inevitable and must be tolerated, but will argue that it can be made more acceptable, and even positively beneficial, provided that everyone has a fair chance of winning, or at least doing well, in the contest for power. Provided that everyone lines up at roughly the same starting point, no one can complain if the race goes to the fleetest of foot. The harsher edges of the neoliberal winner-takes-all approach can be softened, it is fondly hoped, if those who bring up the rear are guaranteed some minimum standards of social support, through some redistribution of wealth and income, and an acceptance of community responsibility for basic services.

The neoliberal, on the other hand, will regard the concentration of power as not only inevitable but positively desirable. According to this view, those who gather power to themselves will be the most able and deserving. And the fact that society is led by the most able will mean that everyone benefits; even the disadvantaged and least powerful will benefit as the rising tide lifts all boats. The possibility, too, that the least powerful can contest for power, and that the exceptionally able or lucky individual might make the breakthrough, will ensure a degree of social mobility and contestability that will maintain the vitality of the system. According to this view, it will be literally counter-productive to try to counteract the concentration of power by ensuring that it is more widely distributed and equally shared. The only consequence would be to drag everyone down to the level of the least able. Contrary to the delusions of the 'third way', the dice must be allowed to lie where they fall. To try to alter the outcome of the game would be to deny the beneficial potency of allowing the winners to prevail.

Historically, the left (or socialists, as we used to say and perhaps should do again) has shared much of the liberal or social democratic agenda, but has evinced less tolerance for the degree of inequality that is inevitably tolerated by that approach. Crucially, only on the left has substantial, entrenched, and often inherited inequality been seen as a straightforward negative, an affront to notions of justice or fairness, a gross limitation on the freedom of the less powerful and therefore of society as a whole, a drag on economic efficiency, a dagger driven at the heart of social cohesion. Only on the left is there an imperative to address the way that power is distributed - and not just redistributed; it is only the left who point out the social and economic price that everyone - including the most powerful - is required to pay for a substantially unequal distribution of power. It is that imperative - to achieve something near equality, not identity - that is the defining characteristic of left politics.

If this is what left politics is really about, what should the left response produce by way of a policy agenda? The first part of the answer to that question concerns the relationship between the market and government, between economic and political power.

Markets and government

No government - of any persuasion - should delude itself as to the critical and irreplaceable role of the market in a modern and democratic economy. At its best, the market allocates scarce resources, empowers consumers (through what might be described as economic democracy), stimulates efficiency and innovation, and rewards the most productive and creative. It is, however, a valuable servant but a dangerous master. It is the elevation of the market to the status of a moral force that cannot be challenged that enables the powerful to by-pass democracy. That view must be contested. If democracy is to mean anything, government must be ready to intervene in the market so that its outcomes are acceptable and sustainable, both politically and economically. The deliberate aim of a left government must be to utilise the market so as to optimise its great strengths, but to make sure as well that the market does not prejudice the wider goal of diffusing power as widely and as fairly as possible throughout society - through entrenching and extending the power of the privileged.

So, good government matters. It is the means by which the market is restrained, so that the full resources of the whole of society are deployed to the widest advantage; by which essential services are provided; by which the economy is managed and directed for the general good; by which the benefits of citizenship are fairly and productively shared; by which the cohesion of society is effectively developed.

This is of course at odds with the right-wing doctrine that government should limit itself to a minimal responsibility for maintaining the value of assets - and particularly the currency - and should otherwise merely hold the ring while market operators are allowed to get on with it. The left has always taken the view that governments are inevitably major players in the economy. They are the most important investors, customers and employers. They influence events and behaviour through policy decisions. As a result, they should accept responsibility for the overall context in which economic activity takes place. They should properly be concerned with the appropriate level of demand, the provision of gainful employment opportunities for all citizens, and the fair distribution of the fruits of economic activity. It was the abandonment of these responsibilities, particularly by the left, that contributed so greatly to the global crisis.

A proper balance between the roles of the market and the government, between economics and democracy, is essential. And it need not - as is often argued - require a sacrifice of economic efficiency for the sake of social outcomes or political principle. The lesson of the last thirty years is that 'free-market' economics do not lead to efficiency - great riches for a tiny minority, yes, but sustained and equitable economic progress for all, no.

The case for diffusing power throughout society is as much economic as it is social. We make the most efficient use of our resources, and particularly of our human resources, if everyone has the chance to make their most appropriate contribution to wealth-creation; if that contribution is fairly recognised and rewarded; if everyone's potential is properly recognised and not suppressed; and if we understand that no individual is so talented as to merit rewards hugely greater than those enjoyed by others, since it is the cumulative effort of the whole of society that is overwhelmingly responsible for the progress we have made.

Soundings

A similar argument can be made concerning the proper use of our natural resources and the sustainability of our environment. If decisions on these matters are taken by democratic agencies answerable to the widest possible constituencies, rather than by a handful of self-interested operators in a short-term market which they dominate, we have a better chance of managing our natural resources to the greatest possible advantage for all of us and of our planet.

These economic and environmental arguments reinforce the great social case for a wider diffusion of power. Freedom in society is not to be measured by the level enjoyed by that powerful minority that benefits from the greatest freedom of choice. Freedom exercised by denying freedom to others - even indirectly, through the supposedly value-free operation of the market - is not the mark of a free society. Only by diffusing power, by breaking down concentrations of power, can we optimise freedom for everyone. The supposed antithesis between freedom and social justice dissolves away when the goal is to allow everyone the maximum level of freedom that is commensurate with a similar level for others.

A society in which power is fairly shared, where everyone has the opportunity to contribute and their contribution is valued and rewarded, and where the benefits of living in society are treated as social goods to which everyone is entitled, will be a society which is cohesive and integrated, which feels good about itself, and which is less likely to display the anti-social behaviour that characterises those marked by alienation and growing inequality.

These principles of democracy, social justice, and community - and the analysis by which those principles are derived - provide us with the basis for deciding an appropriate left political agenda. We should be clear what the touchstones are on issues such as who owns, controls and benefits from the economic process; the appropriate level of guaranteed provision for the basic requirements of a civilised life; what attention should be paid to the interests of others beyond our shores and beyond our lifetimes; and the importance we attach to a sense of fairness for the maintenance of social cohesion and unity.

Signposts for change

The demands of practical politics will inevitably require compromise and trade-offs. But each policy, each new initiative, should meet a sort of health check provided by these touchstones. The alarm bells should ring if the policy agenda is seen to fly in the face of the basic principles. If only New Labour had heard them toll!

Adherence to a body of principle and analysis does not dictate, as is sometimes suggested, a static or backward-looking stance. It will suggest and require adjustments to existing policies as circumstances change. It will inform and stimulate new policy to deal with new issues. It will urge us on to meet the future.

A left agenda framed in this way will exhibit many familiar features, and is none the worse for that. Policies for increasing the stake of ordinary people in wealth creation should feature prominently, as should those for ensuring through redistribution that wealth is shared more fairly, and using the public purse and community responsibility to guarantee the delivery of basic services.

But we should also expect some new thinking to address new issues. A good example is the reappraisal now needed of the value of labour in the economic process. The new reality of labour's declining importance in wealth creation, in comparison with capital-hungry technological advances, means that labour by itself is no longer an adequate basis for a claim to a fair share in society's riches. It may be that it is citizenship, not labour, that should form the basis of that claim, and that we need a new concept of citizenship to help us sustain it. Citizenship is already the basis for a large number of claims on society - equality before the law, the right to vote, and the whole range of human rights; it is not so revolutionary to propose that those basic claims should include a right to a fair share of society's resources.

We will also need a longer timeline and wider horizon than the market can provide if we are serious in our concern for the preservation of our environment and natural resources. Government intervention on behalf of the community is inevitable if we are to inhibit climate change, maintain a fresh and clean water supply, encourage the biodiversity on which our future may depend, and establish a new relationship between humankind and our planet. We need to re-think patterns of land use, methods of food production, and the production and uses of energy. The market can help, but it will be a market that is rigged to produce particular outcomes in the public interest.

In economic terms, we should reclaim economic policy (including monetary policy) as the proper responsibility of democratic government rather than of bankers, and as a proper subject for public debate. We should recognise that economics is a behavioural science and does not lend itself to mechanistic solutions. In particular, we should re-examine the role of the privately owned banks in the light of the current debacle and question whether they should ever again be allowed a virtual monopoly of credit creation. In view of the burden that bank failure has imposed on the taxpayer, should the banking function not be seen as essentially a public responsibility?

The roles of limited liability and the joint-stock company should be re-examined, in view of the irresponsibility and disregard for the public interest that they have demonstrated. New models of industrial ownership and control should be explored, including those that would give working people a stake in their own enterprises.

A left government should take the lead in negotiating new agreements to reform international financial and economic arrangements so that multinational capital takes a more responsible attitude to the communities in which it is invested; the volatility of foreign exchange markets and flows of 'hot money' are restrained; and global imbalances between rich and poor, and between debtor and creditor nations, are addressed effectively.

In social terms, a left government should recognise the over-arching importance of making whole again a society that has been fractured by class, economic circumstance, ethnicity and religion. An inclusive society based on fairness and tolerance, and one that placed a value on all its citizens, would be the most effective antidote to crime and other anti-social behaviour, and would also provide the conditions for improved economic performance. Making full employment once more the prime goal would also be important. An attack on economic inequality through a combination of integrated tax and income support policies would produce a more cohesive society. Health and education services that reflected the public service ethic rather than the profit motive and the market mechanism would also be helpful.

Overseas, a return to Robin Cook's ethical foreign policy would help to restore Britain's standing as a force for good in the world. The same tolerance and inclusivity as was shown domestically would produce similarly constructive results internationally. We should have no more complicity in illegal invasions and torture, or in denials of human rights at home.

Proposals like these are, of course, no more than signposts. They do not by

Constructing a left politics

themselves constitute anything like a comprehensive programme. Rather, they indicate the kind of new - and not so new - thinking that a left agenda that is true to the analysis offered here might encourage. We have the chance to return to our core values and goals, and to update them in the light of events that can now be seen to underpin and validate our approach to politics. We should not miss that opportunity.

The lives of others

Jon Cruddas and Jonathan Rutherford

Philip Collins & Richard Reeves, *The Liberal Republic*, Demos 2009

In the current political turmoil, the political fault-lines of a new era are taking shape. On one side are those who continue to believe that the market and individual choice are the most effective means of maximising individual freedom. On the other side are those who believe that individual freedom is based in social relationships and the democracy of public action. This fault-line cuts across party lines and divides them from within: Thatcherite politics versus Compassionate Conservatism and Red Toryism; market Liberal Democrats versus social Liberal Democrats; neoliberal New Labour versus social democratic Labour.

The fault-line inside the Labour Party has been defined by two groupings: Progress represents the right of centre New Labour establishment, while Compass speaks for an insurgent centre left. But recently a third intervention has been making itself heard. It comes from the think tank Demos, which has been promoting a liberal republican politics. In May it celebrated its sixteenth birthday with the launch of *The Liberal Republic*, co-authored by its chair, Philip Collins, and Director, Richard Reeves (available on www.demos.co.uk).

The authors want to revitalise the liberalism that shaped the New Labour project in its early, idealistic years. Their key themes are the autonomous individual; the radical devolution of power; the value of market choice in distributing freedom; and welfare and public service reform that encourages personal independence. In their brief introduction they outline their conviction that individuals must have the power to determine and create their own version of a good life. 'The good society', they argue, 'is one composed of independent, capable people charting their own course, rather than a perfect shape to be carved by the elite, out of the crooked timber of humanity'. They cite the nineteenth-century liberals Leonard Hobhouse and Thomas Green, and this signals their broader intent: both Hobhouse and Green were involved in the debates between social liberalism and ethical socialism that forged the spirit of the modern left. The pamphlet is an intervention that evokes these earlier debates. It is an overture to the centre left in the form of an invitation to travel back in time to conduct an argument over its conflicting traditions of radical liberalism and socialism.

This invitation comes at a crucial moment for the left, both inside and outside the Labour Party. The Labour Party is teetering on the edge of oblivion and the left is struggling to make a political impact. It lacks a coherent identity, is organisationally and numerically weak, and is unclear about its values. It has no story that defines what it stands for. It has yet to strike a popular chord and transform the centre ground of politics. The self-inflicted crisis of capitalism is serving only to highlight the weakness of the social democratic and liberal left.

If a new progressive politics is to emerge out of this conjuncture of disasters, discussion and new ideas are essential, and this includes re-engaging with earlier traditions and old debates. It is telling that during the last three decades of resurgent capitalism, social democracy in Britain has failed to produce a significant theoretical work to replace Anthony Crosland's *The Future of Socialism*. Crosland's revisionist answer to Marxism, however flawed, at one time provided an intellectual cornerstone for the centre left. Crosland was always out there on the horizon, keeping alive the language of class, capitalism and equality, a beacon of hope that social democracy would one day pay off. But Crosland's model of social democracy was dealt a near fatal blow in 1976 when the Labour government abandoned the post-war welfare consensus and was forced cap in hand to the IMF. Any flames of the beacon left flickering after the rise of the Third Way were finally extinguished by the post-crash budget of April 2009. The left needs to forge a new politics and develop theoretical ideas for these changed times. Has liberal republicanism something to offer?

The social individual

The authors of *The Liberal Republic* are confident that the future lies in the historical legacy of liberalism and its modern kindred spirits. The work of Amartya Sen plays a central role in their social policy ideas. As they acknowledge, the conditions for a self-directed life do not emerge out of thin air: 'independence requires a set of what Amartya Sen labels capabilities - especially financial resources, education and skills and health. Without them the goal of independence is a pipe dream'. They recognise that to ensure these capabilities a correction must be made in the current extremely low level of benefits, and the unequal distribution of wealth and assets. They also acknowledge that the low pay of a large proportion of the working population is insufficient to support an autonomous life. Similarly, there is a need to increase taxes on unearned financial resources and inherited wealth, because this will promote independence. They also support electoral reform and the devolution of power into the hands of the people. Liberalism means individuals becoming the authors of their own lives, 'but republicanism demands that we are also co-authors of our collective lives' (p57).

These views belong to a centre left politics - Hobhouse and Green would not dissent from them. But the problems begin when the nature of this co-authorship is probed: their ideas on how to achieve a good society are not convincing. Their liberalism dominates their republicanism and they have little to say about a collective politics of change. Their call for power to the people is limited, and mirrors David Cameron's vague idea of a post-bureaucratic society: 'The best way of describing what we are suggesting is that it is a revolutionary transfer of power from one class, the bureaucracy, to another, the people' (p47). There is no mention of making the power of employers accountable, or of dispersing power in economic institutions. They are not concerned by the 'gap between the affluent and the "super-rich"'. They do not think that wealth inequality threatens political equality and do not see why the 'mega-incomes of a handful of people' should 'prevent the rest of us leading a good life' (p35). Unlike the social liberals, they offer no conception of the common good (or of society, or of community) that recognises the interdependency of individuals. They have nothing to say about the role of culture in binding people together and creating identity out of shared meanings. What holds their liberal social order together? Friedrich von Hayek would argue that it is the economic relations of the market. Philip and Richard insist that their liberal economics is not the same as neoliberal economics - but they do not explain why. At the heart of their political philosophy is the absence of the social realm. And this is the fundamental weakness in their argument.

'The beginning of a liberal politics is the individual', they write. But what is their

Reviews

definition of an individual? Richard and Philip take this question for granted, and treat the individual as a discrete, historically unchanging unit, governed by rational thinking. But as Marx pointed out many years ago, liberal political economists are mistaken in seeing the individual as history's point of departure rather than its historic result. As he argued, the modern epoch that produces the isolated individual is also the epoch of the most developed social relations. The individual is a sociological category, made in a complexity of emotional, cultural and economic relations. But Richard and Philip's liberal philosophy ignores this complexity. They comment that not everyone will be successful in life: 'Our lives may be wracked with tragedy and failure - but they are our own tragedies and failures' (p9). But they do not recognise that, though as individuals we may often be the architects of our own downfall, we do not control the broader conditions that give rise to our tragedies and failures.

We have no choice about the class, family, race and gender we are born into - and which will define our life chances. We do not decide the inequalities which determine the prospects of our longevity, the statistical likelihood of our succumbing to poverty, poor housing, unemployment, murder, prison, disease, mental illness, obesity, educational failure. Very few of us can influence the hierarchies of status which trigger the social emotions of shame and humiliation that impact on our well-being from the beginning of our lives. These are socially produced problems of class and economic power and they require collective action to change. Challenging them cannot be the responsibility of individuals alone - as has been the pernicious message of market fundamentalists. But the authors mobilise Sen's concept of capability as a means of disconnecting the social from their argument, and in their zealous advocacy of individual 'independence' they end up perpetuating the anti-politics of neoliberalism.

This is particularly evident in their uncritical promotion of the government's welfare reforms, and its personalisation agenda in social care. They make unsubstantiated claims such as: 'individual budgets give *control* to the citizen'; and 'recipients are happier, results are better and costs lower' (p49). For them welfare reform is defined by the problem of recipients who are 'unable to do without state handouts'. They consider this inability an immoral condition, that demands correction through conditionality in the benefits system: after one year recipients should work full time for their benefits. John Stuart Mill is called on to endorse this 'liberation welfare'. They quote his comment that welfare assistance 'should be a tonic, not a sedative' (p17). But they get the quote wrong. Mill said 'assistance *is a* tonic, not a sedative' - for people who are discouraged.

Politics and sympathy

Why are the authors concerned with the lives of others? What compels them to worry about the independence of strangers? Their take on liberal philosophy offers us no clues - but their politics is not driven by sympathy, or any sense of ethical obligation. Though they cite Hobhouse, they do not share his social liberalism. For Hobhouse, progress is 'the development of that rational organization of life in which men freely recognise their interdependence, and the best life for each is understood to be that which is best for those around him' (*The Ethical Basis of Collectivism*, p150). But the notion of freedom espoused in this pamphlet carries with it an element of moral coercion. Its liberalism slips its social moorings as the authors assert a series of absolutes: 'people should not be dependent on anyone else for their income'; 'there can never be agreement about the values and purposes of life' (p21). There is an underlying moral imperative that individuals must maximise their independence from the state, must free themselves from conditions of dependency and must follow that 'most human attribute', the ability to choose.

Despite its claim to a social liberalism, *The Liberal Republic* is about creating market actors capable of functioning in a market society governed by individual rational choice. Its frame of reference can best be understood as consonant with the kind of liberal form of governance analysed by Michel Foucault - one that uses indirect techniques for controlling individuals without at the same time being responsible for them. In this form of governance a coercive and interventionist state creates the institutions the market needs, and attempts to shape the character of individuals.

In their advocacy of welfare reform, Richard and Philip echo the utilitarian liberalism of Jeremy Bentham, who, in respect of welfare, was a believer in firm government: for him the influence of legislation was 'as nothing' in comparison with the 'minister of police'. Mill described Bentham as a man who had no sympathy. There is a callousness in Benthamite and economic liberalism, and it is present in *The Liberal Republic*. (Mill himself struggled with the absence of empathy in his own life: he discovered it in the romantic poetry of Coleridge, and in the person of his wife, Harriet Taylor. But he could not make it a part of his own self, and was unable to synthesise the emotional and rational in his liberal philosophy.) Phillip and Richard allow their liberal rationalism to dominate over any kind of emotional identification that embraces others in a mutual recognition. Nothing holds their social order together except the moral imperative to maximise personal autonomy.

Ethical socialism also begins with the individual, but it is with the social individual relating to others and producing in society. The central value of socialism, alongside liberty, is equality, because, as Hobhouse writes, 'it stands for the truth that there is a common humanity deeper than all our superficial distinctions' (p141). Socialism is about the structure of relations between individuals, which shape both our psyche and our place in the world. It does not pitch the individual against society, but sees individuals as constituted in society. Society has its own kind of regularity, but it is nothing more than the relationships of individuals. There is no 'I' without first a 'we' that is historical and forged out of culture and society.

Unlike liberalism, ethical socialism is based on a mutual recognition between individuals: 'your freedom is equal to my own'. It asserts an 'ethical intention' in the sphere of politics. Paul Ricoeur describes this as 'the desire to live well with and for others in just institutions'. The scandal of MPs' expenses and the public fury it has unleashed suggests a society that has forgotten this concept of politics. Ethical values have given way to a culture of individual self-interest in which those who have feel entitled to take more. Power is unaccountable, and the political elites are divorced from the people. The enterprise culture, the flexible labour market and welfare reform have all generated anxiety and isolation rather than 'independence'. The state of dependency that is the precondition for self-reliance has been held in contempt by tabloids and politicians alike. Those on benefits have been demonised. In public service, kindness, care, generosity and reciprocity are out of keeping with the dominant market culture and are micro-managed out of existence. A public culture of distrust and resentment is the legacy of decades of neoliberalism and the inequalities and erosion of social bonds that it has caused.

The liberal individualism of *The Liberal Republic* is unlikely to remedy this condition. Two institutions have dominated the life of this country for the last thirty years: the state and the market. How shall we reform them, in order to confront the massive systemic problems we face? The progressive future belongs to those who find a credible answer to this question, and who are able to achieve a popular balance between individual self-realisation and social solidarity. The politics of the future needs to revisit the old arguments between liberalism and socialism, and incorporate into them the issues of gender inequality, cultural difference and ecological sustainability. This will involve alliances between old and new political actors. What shape it takes, and what it might be called, are not yet clear - but *The Liberal Republic* seems to have placed itself outside this epoch-defining debate.

No small undertaking

Sofi Charlstan

Pat Devine, Andrew Pearmain and David Purdy (eds) *Feelbad Britain: How to make it better*, Lawrence & Wishart 2009

Feelbad Britain is a revision of an essay of the same name originally published in February 2007, complemented this time around with a series of additional essays which further develop some of the main strands of the argument. The authors of the main essay describe themselves as people who have each been involved in left-wing politics for upwards of forty years; their objective is to bring an historical understanding and a Gramscian perspective to bear on the analysis of what has gone wrong with British society and what we need to do to fix it. Given the disintegration of left-wing politics in this country, our petty floundering in the face of climate change, and the growing social and economic polarisation of our society, if there was ever a time for wisdoms and historical insights to inform the task ahead, it is probably now.

Our social recession

The book begins with a few cold hard facts and a summary of the evidence of the pretty dire state of Britain's social fabric. Firstly, as widely argued in recent years, despite increasing wealth and material prosperity, people are on average no happier than they were twenty to thirty years ago. Far more concerning though, is the widespread incidence of clinical depression and anxiety, and the steep rise in the incidence of

Reviews

depression in children since the 1970s. Added to that is the increase in inequality, begun under Thatcher and unhalted by New Labour, which means that Britain is now more unequal in terms of income than in any year since 1961, when statistics were first published. And then there's the reduction of social mobility, with a contraction in opportunities for working-class kids whilst 'old boys' style middle-class networks have consolidated in growth industries like banking and new media. We have more people in prison than ever, including the highest population of children in prison in the western world, and the highest rate of premature birth in Europe. And last but not least, there's our unprecedented levels of anxiety-inducing personal indebtedness, driven by the irresponsible lending of the banks and contributing to the current economic crisis.

As well as looking at the ways in which market forces and values have corroded our well-being and social relations, the authors also, perhaps more interestingly, look at other tendencies and impulses inherited by New Labour from Thatcherism. Two of these are New Labour's growing authoritarianism and centralisation of power; and its singling out of groups within British society as scapegoats for the hardships and unhappiness neoliberalism has inflicted on the masses. After some initial toying with devolution, New Labour adopted the same approach to centres of power outside of central government as Thatcher had done: it focused on weakening and undermining every main source of political legitimacy and involvement outside of central government - from local councils to trade unions to professional bodies - and on the consolidation of that power centrally. From undermining teachers, to extending financial control over local authorities, New Labour has sought to delegitimise and corrode what remained of the nexuses of public participation in the governance and reproduction of our society. This has undermined what the authors describe as our 'system of social citizenship', turning many people who were once more active in governing or operating their local social infrastructure into passive consumers, and recipients of services controlled by bureaucrats who are both physically and socially remote.

New Labour has also wholeheartedly adopted Thatcherism's invocation of rhetorical enemies of the state to divert attention away from the real forces and agents corroding our social and economic wellbeing. Muslims, hoodies and immigrants have joined the classic and ubiquitous Thatcherite character of the 'scrounger' as the principal targets of poisonous rhetoric espoused by government. And while British society has been busy hating immigrants and scroungers, the process of elite self-enrichment has continued, with ever bigger bonuses not just for big business fat cats but also for the newly installed quango and public sector elite. And on top of this the delegitimisation of professionals and weakening of local authorities and other centres of power has smoothed the way for the further privatisation of public services and the replacement of the ethos of public service with market principles.

Policy-itis and insights from Gramsci

From the point of view of the authors, Gramsci is key to understanding why the above-described processes have continued under New Labour: specifically through his concepts of hegemony and 'transformism'. In Gramscian theory, politics takes the form of a struggle for hegemony, in which different classes seek to present their interests as the interest of all and thereby establish their claim to leadership over a whole society (p33). Successful hegemony requires the building of alliances, with the objective of constructing a 'historic bloc' of social forces, gathered around a dominant class and held together by that class's hegemonic ideology, which then becomes 'the common sense of the age' (p34). On this approach, the ascendancy of the neoliberal right in the 1970s was not merely opportunism but rather a political project aimed at achieving social, political and economic change in the long run, and underpinned by a coherent ideological basis. However, its project eventually unravelled, with the social breakdown of the 1980s leading to outright civil disorder and necessitating a tweaking and rebranding. Enter New Labour.

In contrast to Thatcherism, it is argued that New Labour has never had a long-term project. Rather, New Labour government is seen as afflicted by 'a kind of policy-itis, an epidemic of proposals and targets and executive summaries'. It assumes 'a kind of Attention Deficit Disorder on the part of the British public' (p70). This focus on superficiality, spin and the rapid deployment of new policies is a necessary cover for the absence of any underlying strategy or set of values beyond the continuation of the Thatcherite drive to extend the reach and rule of the market whatever the cost.

Some political grounding for a new generation?

Feelbad Britain definitely fills a big gap. The fact that the authors felt the need to write it also begs some interesting questions, including why so many new political activists are so out of touch with political history and theory, and the experiences and learnings

Reviews

of the movements that have gone before them. Are we experiencing a low-point in political consciousness, itself a product of thirty years of neoliberal capitalism and the degradation of our social fabric?

What is also very interesting is that the authors broach certain 'no go areas' which we need to face up to if the democratic left is to have even the remotest chance of launching a truly transformational project of its own. The critique of the militant labourism of the trade unions in the 1970s is one such discussion. Similarly, *Feelbad Britain* refreshingly acknowledges the big problems with the state-owned enterprises of the post-war era, which were not subject to democratic control any more than private-owned enterprises are. They also offer an interesting and poignant critique of green politics, touching on the long-standing philosophical gulf that exists within the environmental movement between those who are motivated by what they believe to be the intrinsic value of nature and those who are primarily concerned about protecting the environment *for* people. They assert the need for the green movement to get over its privileging of the traditional and the rural and to get to grips with the modern age:

> Green politics needs to focus on the social as well as the
> environmental, and on ways of involving as well as alarming people,
> two political techniques that do not always sit comfortably together.
> It also needs to celebrate rather than oppose the modern and the
> urban, to engage with the popular mainstream as well as the variously
> disaffected, and to demonstrate that a sustainable society and lifestyle
> would offer a better, not worse, quality of life (p73).

There is a risk that a book like this might take a rose-tinted view of the past, a bit like your grandma harking back to the good old days - a golden age when you spoke to your neighbours and didn't lock your back door - whilst conveniently forgetting the suffocating nature of community life in post-war Britain and the stigmas and prejudices that cast many to the edges of society. Fortunately *Feelbad Britain* resists any such romanticisation; their point is that neoliberalism has brought out the worst in us, and that New Labour hasn't done very much to make things better.

The editors of *Feelbad Britain* hold out little hope for the transformation of the Labour Party as the solution to the current void on the democratic left, asserting that as an institution it is now geared entirely to the support of career politicians backed by special interests and that the central control exerted within it make prospects for successful political change from the inside pretty bleak.

They also seek to manage our expectations about the immensity of the task ahead, however, arguing that the kind of transformation that is needed in the social, political and economic spheres is unlikely to be achieved straightforwardly, or in our lifetimes, because of the fundamental cultural change needed first; namely the growth of desire for more participatory forms of democracy in the first place. They helpfully point to a few ideas to start us off, and these are elaborated in the essays that follow. One of the most interesting proposals is the one simply stated in the main essay - that the project which drives forward the campaigns for these solutions must be a diverse one, undertaken by a 'rainbow alliance' comprising all the various components of the left outside of the Parliamentary Labour Party. Some guidance from the authors on how to construct such an alliance wouldn't go amiss, though, given the current tendency for many organisations in this space to compete against one another, and the clamouring amongst them to become the banner under which the democratic left unites. Perhaps the authors are leaving that one for the next political generation to work out.

Better on symptoms than remedies

David Purdy

Jesse Norman, *Compassionate Economics*, Policy Exchange and the University of Buckingham Press Ltd, 2008

Jesse Norman is a Senior Fellow and former Executive Director of Policy Exchange. He is also the Conservative Party candidate for Hereford and South Herefordshire. This short book is the second part of a larger project aimed at providing a coherent intellectual and practical basis for the New Conservatism (available on-line at www.ubpl.co.uk).. The first part, published in 2006 under the title *Compassionate Conservatism*, traces the historical roots of this project and develops the concept of the 'connected society', a term intended to shift attention away from the 'vertical' relations between individuals and the state which have preoccupied political thinkers since Hobbes, towards a 'horizontal' concern with social institutions and human relationships

It would be a mistake to dismiss compassionate conservatism simply because the badge was once worn by George W. Bush. Neither 'Red Tories' such as Phillip Blond nor 'Tory Whigs' such as Jesse Norman have anything in common with the US neo-cons. Rather, at a time when the New Labour project lies in ruins and the temple of neoliberalism is badly damaged (though far from destroyed), these New Conservatives are openly critical of certain aspects of the Thatcher revolution, seriously concerned about Britain's 'broken society', and eager to remind their fellow Conservatives of their party's intellectual heritage, from Burke's organic view of society to Carlyle's polemics against laissez-faire capitalism and Ruskin's critique of liberal political economy. Not surprisingly, given this provenance, many of the criticisms that 'red' or 'compassionate' Tories level at New Labour and mainstream economics echo those made by the democratic left, certainly as regards the symptoms of Britain's social crisis and even in terms of basic values, though as I argue later, they misdiagnose the state we are in and their proposed remedies are unconvincing, not least because if the Conservatives win next year's general election and take an axe to public spending at a time when GDP has stopped falling but recovery is by no means assured, the resulting economic hardship is likely to damage social cohesion still further.

The argument of *Compassionate Economics* is that even before the onset of the great recession in the autumn of 2008, the UK's economic performance since 1993 had flattered to deceive. It looked good compared with the crisis-torn 1970s, the recession-wracked 1980s and the sclerosis that afflicted the eurozone in the 1990s. But in fact, the UK grew more slowly than other rich, free-market, Anglophone economies and its growth was driven by simultaneous booms in government spending, immigration, house price inflation and personal debt, against a backdrop of low interest rates and easy credit, all ephemeral factors that did nothing to strengthen the underlying foundations of prosperity: productivity, social institutions and the education system. Indeed, the multiple social disorders that accompanied Britain's debt-fuelled spending spree, manifested in levels of drug abuse, binge drinking, teenage pregnancy, family breakdown and child mental illness that are far worse than those found in other affluent countries, suggest a society which is deeply troubled and dysfunctional.

Norman attributes both the flawed economic boom and the unfolding social crisis to the malign influence of what he calls the standard economic model, sometimes known as 'rigor mortis economics', a body of ideas about markets and government which over the past forty years has not only dominated the teaching of economics and the conduct of public policy, but has even taken root in everyday life. The model, a sophisticated mathematical construct based on the assumption that all economic agents - individual persons, commercial firms and public agencies alike - are self-interested rational maximisers, describes the operation of an idealised competitive market economy in abstraction from any specific form of social life and uses deductive reasoning to demonstrate that, if it existed, such a system would satisfy people's wants and preferences to the maximum extent and at the lowest cost possible, given available resources and technology. Questions of distribution - who owns what, who gets what and whether the rules of the game are fair - are a separate matter on which economists qua economists make no comment. They do, however, concede that wherever actual markets deviate from the ideal conditions assumed in the model, the resulting 'market failure' creates a prima facie case for government intervention to produce an outcome closer to the optimum, as if the fault lies in reality, not the model.

There is, as Norman notes, abundant evidence that people do not behave as rational economic maximisers: they are, for example, biased towards the present and the status quo, even in the face of incentives to change; they do not systematically evaluate alternatives; they are influenced by the way choices are framed; and their motivations are not reducible to the lure of gain or the fear of loss. Neither does the standard model do justice to the dynamic, liquid character of real markets, understood as historically evolved and culturally embedded forms of social interaction; while the concept of market failure is so elastic as to give government almost unlimited licence to intervene. And the effect of ignoring social institutions and relationships is to establish a presumption in favour of centralisation and the command-and-control mentality which, when applied to the public services, has done untold harm, lowering professional morale, undermining public trust, and creating a whole new layer of officialdom to monitor, inspect and audit the performance of public agencies.

Norman singles out the tax credit system devised by Gordon Brown and administered by the Treasury as a particularly egregious instance of centralised, over-complex and wasteful micro-management, which few people understand and which, far from enhancing income security, causes anxiety and hardship whenever (as happens all too frequently) claimants are overpaid and the authorities subsequently demand repayment. This said, he fails to explain why the government opted for this particular anti-poverty policy rather than any other, and offers no preferred alternative of his own. It is also worth noting that tax-credits are descended from the idea of a Negative Income Tax, proposed by Milton Friedman in 1962, with cavalier disregard for the problems of implementation that always arise in connection with plans for reforming social security.

Much of what is wrong with received economic theory stems from its impoverished conception of the person. Stripped of their social characteristics and abstracted from the cultural settings that give shape and meaning to their lives, human individuals become atomised bearers of wants and preferences, mere vessels for transient experiences of pleasure and pain. In place of this solitary, passive and hedonistic conception of the self, Norman commends a view of the person as an active, autonomous acquirer and exerciser of capabilities, changing and developing over time, involved in a variety of social relationships and constantly seeking outlets for self-expression.

The active self is one aspect of compassionate economics, with far-reaching implications for the education system. The other is what Norman calls the social foundations of economic prosperity: a flourishing civil society; a judicious blend of competition and co-operation; and a vigorous entrepreneurial spirit, broadly understood in terms of open-minded inquiry and creative thinking, not simply as having an eye for the main chance. The financial crash of 2008 forces us to rethink economic theory and policy from the ground up. Compassionate economics is not a new set of policies, but a new paradigm, a set of guidelines for producing policies. Norman claims that if this paradigm becomes established in public discourse and institutional reform, it holds out the promise of replacing the kind of casino capitalism that has evolved in Britain over the past thirty years with a more solid, stable and civilised variety.

Soundings

As indicated earlier, the democratic left can happily endorse much of this argument. Critics of neo-classical economics have long complained that it treats human individuals as asocial atoms and that its understanding of the market is ludicrously mechanistic. And the concept of the active, developing self should commend itself to anyone who subscribes to the ideals of personal autonomy and participatory democracy, for only people who are capable of thinking for themselves and making their own reflective choices and decisions will have the capacity and desire to participate in the business of governing, including the governing of business.

Neoclassical economics undoubtedly helped to shape the mindset and policies that have brought Western capitalism in general, and Britain in particular, to their present parlous condition. The prime culprit, however, is not the standard economic model, but rather the neoliberal political project which it helped to inspire and legitimise.

Neoliberalism - a term, incidentally, which is conspicuous by its absence from Norman's account - was forged in opposition to Keynesian social democracy, the fusion of social democratic politics and Keynesian economics that governed public policy during the 'golden age' of post-war capitalism from 1945 to 1975. But neoliberalism was always more than a recipe for quelling inflation, corralling the public sector, replenishing corporate profits and restoring the primacy of market forces in economic life. Behind its harsh remedies for the economic failings of the old regime, lay the idea that the good society is one in which individuals enjoy maximum (and, in principle, equal) freedom to seek their own salvation in their own way so long as they do no harm to others. According to neoliberals, the form of society that best enshrines this ideal is one based on private ownership of productive assets, free contracts, competitive markets, commercial money and generalised commodity production. The only legitimate role of government is to establish (or re-establish) the institutions and norms that underpin these conditions.

Neoclassical economics was only one of the sources and component parts of the neoliberal project. The others, in no particular order of importance, were Hayek's restatement of classical liberalism and the Austrian tradition of economic thought; Chicago monetarism, as expounded by Milton Friedman; and the theory of public choice developed in the 1960s by writers such as James Buchanan, who sought to apply the model of *homo economicus* to the behaviour of governments, bureaucracies and voters. To be sure, these diverse schools of thought are not altogether compatible. There is, in particular, a major theoretical disagreement between neo-classical economists, who equate uncertainty with risk and seek to show how market forces steer the economy towards a state of general equilibrium (a concept borrowed from Newtonian physics), and their Austrian rivals, who see the market as a framework for trial, error, discovery and innovation and have no time for the concept of equilibrium. But political projects, unlike logical arguments or scientific theories, do not need to be totally free from inconsistency: indeed, up to a point, internal tensions are a source of strength. At the end of the second world war, for example, the policy paradigm we now call Keynesian social democracy appealed to liberal collectivists and one-nation conservatives, as well as to social democrats. Similarly, when this paradigm proved incapable of resolving the organic crisis of the 1970s, neoliberalism provided a rallying point for all those who wanted to dismantle the post-war settlement and found a new kind of state.

Now that the neoliberal project in turn is in crisis, the challenge is to promote economic recovery, rebuild social cohesion and combat global warming, all at the same time. Norman has nothing to say about environmental issues, and although he recognises the gravity of Britain's social problems, he appears to share the Tory leadership's view that our best hope of escaping from recession is to reduce the scale of public borrowing by cutting public expenditure, a policy which could easily cut short any incipient economic upturn and plunge us into a 1930s-style depression. This is not to deny that Keynesian reflation poses difficult problems of public finance. Nevertheless, in a situation where capitalism has come to the end of a long consumer boom and cannot be revived by efforts to get the private sector to take on yet more debt, it is better for government to act as 'spender of last resort' than to wait for market forces to engender a 'spontaneous recovery', a process that could take many years and would do nothing to combat climate change, but would almost certainly exacerbate Britain's social decline.

From this standpoint, our best hope lies in a green new deal, focusing on projects which are centrally sponsored and financed, but locally planned and implemented, and which bring together central government, local authorities and civil society in a concerted effort to cut carbon emissions, conserve energy and increase energy efficiency. Indeed, the revival of social hope and the emulation of Obama's 'can do' politics could rekindle what Keynes called the 'animal spirits' of enterprise - the will to act and create without knowing for certain whether the venture will succeed - thereby re-stimulating private investment and reducing the need for deficit-financed public spending.

Notes on contributors

Guy Brown is a lecturer at the University of Cambridge, and does research on cell death and degenerative disease. His most recent book is *The Living End: The Future of Death, Aging and Immortality*, Palgrave-Macmillan 2007.

Julia Buxton is a Senior Research Fellow in the Centre for International Cooperation and Security in the Department of Peace Studies at the University of Bradford. She is the author of *The Political Economy of Narcotics: Production, Consumption and Global Markets*, Zed Books 2006, and editor of the forthcoming *The Politics of Drugs*, Routledge 2009.

Sofi Charlstan works as a campaigner and activist as part of the environmental and global justice movement.

Hilary Cottam is a founder of Participle, designing services with and for the public. Beveridge 4.0 is available on line at www.participle.net

Jon Cruddas is MP for Dagenham and co-editor of *Is the Future Conservative?*; and *The Crash - a view from the left*, both available at www.soundings.org.uk.

Tim Dartington is a writer and social researcher working with health and social welfare agencies. He trained at the Tavistock Institute, carrying out action research studies of the care of older people, of those with physical disabilities, and of children in hospital. He continues to work on issues of vulnerability in contemporary society.

Bryan Gould was elected as Labour MP for Dagenham in 1983 and joined the Shadow Cabinet in 1986. He directed Labour's election campaign in 1987, and contested the Labour Party leadership in 1992. In 1994 he returned to New Zealand as Vice-Chancellor of Waikato University. He is currently a director of Television New Zealand. His website is http://www. bryangould.net/.

notes on contributors

Ben Little is an associate lecturer in the Media Department at Middlesex University, where he teaches campaigning to first year undergraduates. His PhD dealt in part with the cultural convergence that took place in British and American popular culture in the 1980s. He considers himself part of the millennial generation and voted for Ken Livingstone.

Robin Maynard has worked for more than twenty years in the environment movement, including posts as FOE's Countryside & Agriculture campaigner and later as Director of Local Campaigns; with FARM; and as Campaigns Director at the Soil Association.

David Purdy is a social economist and a member of Democratic Left Scotland. He is a co-editor of *Feelbad Britain*, Lawrence and Wishart 2009.

Sarah Radcliffe teaches at the University of Cambridge, and researches social development in Latin America. She is author (with R. Andolina and N. Laurie) of *Indigenous Development in the Andes: Power, culture and transnationalism*, Duke University Press, forthcoming.

Jonathan Rutherford is editor of *Soundings*.

Göran Therborn is Professor of Sociology at Cambridge University. His latest books include (as editor and co-author) *Inequalities of the World* (Verso); and *Between Sex and Power. Family in the World 1900-2000* (Routledge).

Jane Wills is Professor of Geography at Queen Mary, University of London. Recent research projects include an exploration of the role and significance of migrant workers in low-paid employment in London and a study of the London living wage campaign. Her university department is an active member of London Citizens. Her forthcoming book, written with colleagues, is *Global Cities at Work: New migrant divisions of labour*, Pluto Press 2009.

Karel Williams is director of the ESRC funded Centre for Research in Socio Cultural

Change at the University of Manchester (cresc.ac.uk). He works with a team of researchers on the growing influence of finance in present day capitalism; the results include two major books: Julie Froud, Sukhdev Johal, Adam Leaver, Karel Williams, *Financialization and Strategy*, Routledge 2006; and Ismail Erturk, Julie Froud, Sukhdev Johal, Adam Leaver, Karel Williams, *Financialization at Work*, Routledge 2008.

Terry Wrigley is the author of three books on educational change: *The Power to Learn*, Trentham Books 2000; *Schools of Hope*, Trentham Books 2003; and *Another School is Possible*, Trentham Books 2006. He edits the international journal *Improving Schools* (Sage). He is a senior lecturer in education at the University of Edinburgh.

Breaking up Britain:
Four nations after a Union

Mark Perryman (editor)

'This brilliant book helps us understand what Scots, Welsh, Irish and English neighbours, freed from an unhappy Union, might look like.' - Billy Bragg

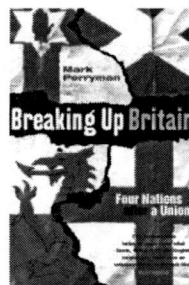

May 2009 marked the tenth anniversary of the first elections to the Scottish Parliament and Welsh Assembly. This was the beginning of a decade of change - which now includes the restoration of powers to Stormont - that is showing every sign of being an irreversible process. *Breaking Up Britain* is a unique collection of English, Scottish, Welsh and Irish contributors, who each explore the change that the break-up demands in their own nation, as well as its impact upon the whole.

Contributors: *Gerry Adams, Arthur Aughey, Gregor Gall, John Harris, Michael Kenny, Peadar Kirby, Guy Lodge, Inez McCormack, John Osmond, Mike Parker, Lesley Riddoch, Richard Thomson, Vron Ware, Charlotte Williams, Kevin Williamson, Leanne Wood and Salma Yaqoob.*

Feelbad Britain:
How to make it better
Pat Devine, Andrew Pearmain and David Purdy (editors)

Contemporary British society is in a troubled and dysfunctional state, without the cohesion or confidence needed if we are to escape from recession, combat climate change and restore faith in government. The authors put forward a theoretical framework for understanding contemporary politics; and consider what is to be done to revitalise the British left, challenge neoliberal hegemony, and develop a political project aimed at creating a greener, fairer, happier, more democratic and less divided Britain.

Contributors: *Patrick Ainley, Martin Allen, David Beetham, Noel Castree, Pat Devine, Angela McRobbie, Linda Patterson, Andrew Pearmain, Michael Prior, David Purdy, Kate Soper*

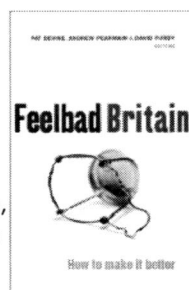

All L&W books available from www.lwbooks.co.uk

Soundings

Soundings
A journal of politics and culture
Issue 42 Summer 2009

'*Soundings* is defining the new politics - spread the word'

Jon Cruddas MP

The killing fields of inequality

Recent themes have included: recession economics, the personalisation agenda, international politics, cultures of capitalism, wellbeing, the future of the left

Soundings is thinking ahead

To subscribe and for more information about *Soundings*, including access to many free-to-view articles, go to http://www.books.co.uk/journals/soundings/contents.html